D1385579

If you like playing, watching, or just reading about soccer, you'll find plenty to entertain you in this book. There's lots of useful advice on choosing your position on the field and improving your game, plus helpful hints on buying and looking after your equipment, as well as a chapter of amazing facts about football and a brief history of the game. Phil Parkes gives a few words of introduction and there are plenty of pictures and diagrams from start to finish.

Tom Tully is well known as a writer of sports stories and picture stories, and is the author of Roy of the Rovers. He takes an active interest in sport, and his favourite football team is Newcastle.

# Football

## A Complete Guide to Better Soccer

### Tom Tully

*Illustrated by Mike Jackson*
*Cartoons by David Mostyn*

SEVERN HOUSE

First British hardcover edition published 1980
by SEVERN HOUSE PUBLISHERS LTD
144–146 New Bond Street, London W1Y 9FD
with acknowledgment to the Hamlyn Publishing Group Ltd

Originally published in paperback under the title
*'The Beaver Book of Football'*

My thanks to George Mills, Roy Merryweather,
John Wood Sports, Horst Juergens and, of
course, Phil Parkes, for help and information in
writing this book.

T.T.

British Library Cataloguing in Publication Data
Tully, Tom
Football.
1. Soccer – Juvenile literature
I. Title
796.334 GV943.25
ISBN 0 7278 0685 8

Printed in Great Britain by The Anchor Press Ltd
and bound by Wm Brendon & Son Ltd
both of Tiptree, Essex

# Contents

# Foreword by Phil Parkes

Every now and then things happen in the football world which take everyone by surprise; and that includes long-serving professionals, such as myself. When I was asked to write the foreword for this book, I was a Queens Park Rangers player, deeply involved with my team-mates in the battle to avoid relegation to the Second Division of the English Football League. By the time I actually sat down to write the foreword, a few days later, I had been transferred across London to West Ham United, and found myself fighting for promotion back into the First Division!

Such is the speed at which things can happen, and this is what makes football such an interesting and unpredictable game. And that is how I would describe *The Beaver Book of Football* – interesting and unpredictable. It brings a welcome breath of fresh air to the multitude of books which have been written about soccer. Combining humour with expert advice, this book is designed to help younger players improve their skills, and expand their knowledge of the game. Even I was fascinated by the author's 'Mine of Information'. The chapters on technique come across clearly and simply, with Cool Kevin and Pushy Pete showing us in a light-hearted but sensible way how things should and shouldn't be done.

I am sure that footballers from the age of 5 to 35 will be able to learn something from this book. Always remember that you can never know too much about football. Listen to your coaches, watch as many top-class games as you can, and be willing to learn. I have been a professional for ten years, and I am still learning.

Football has been described as the greatest game in the world. It's certainly a game that rewards dedication and honesty. So enjoy yourself, keep practising, and one of these days you might just find yourself the subject of a transfer deal that takes the world of football by surprise! Good luck, and best wishes,

# 1 ABOUT THE BOOK

*Another* book about football? That's right . . . but we're hoping that you will find this one a little different from all the others.

There are, of course, the usual illustrated chapters dealing with the basic skills and techniques. If you dream of becoming a professional we give you a fascinating 'back-stage' glimpse into the life of an apprentice. On the other hand, if all you require is a little help in improving your game – thereby increasing your enjoyment of soccer – Chapter 6 outlines a number of simple, entertaining practices that you can try on your own or with a friend. Chapter 9 contains some useful advice on buying and maintaining equipment, whereas the section called 'A mine of information' will be of interest to anyone who is fascinated by the facts and figures of football.

Perhaps you fancy the idea of becoming a referee? If so, you'll find all the information you need in Chapter 8. Other chapters cover the intriguing origins of Soccer; the World Cup competition; and we even take a look at the incredible and colourful progress of the game in America.

And if you like a few 'fun-spots' with your football, you'll find Pushy Pete and Cool Kevin, helping to raise a chuckle along the way.

Pete is the scruffy one – the noisy, aggressive Know-All who will surely reach the top once his 'talents' have been recognised. Kevin is the player who listens and learns. He does the simple things calmly and correctly, with consideration for others.

Kevin also realises that the true soccer enthusiast comes in all shapes and sizes and shades of skill. So whether you play, organise, or just like to watch our game of soccer, we hope that you will find something to interest and excite you in *The Beaver Book of Football.*

# 2 THE BASIC SKILLS

Ask any soccer manager to define a 'good footballer', and he will probably think long and hard before giving you an answer. Pele of Brazil, Di Stefano of Real Madrid and Bobby Charlton of Manchester United and England were all good players ... but for very different reasons. There is no magic 'formula' for success at football. You can only become a better player than you are now by practising hard to improve your skills. And you will never make any real progress in the game until you can kick a football correctly.

## Kicking the ball

Some beginners can kick a ball correctly through sheer instinct. But most of us, like Pushy Pete, have to master this fundamental technique through hours of patient practice. Even experienced professionals are sometimes put through special kicking and shooting sessions, just to remind them how it's done! As we shall see, there are various types of kicks, and passes. But it is best to forget all about them until you have learned to strike a football correctly with your *instep*.

Let's assume that the

ball is stationary. Place your non-kicking foot alongside the ball, with the body leaning forward so that your head is over the ball (fig. 1a). As your kicking foot swings at the ball, slightly from the side, keep your toe pointing down (fig. 1b), so that you strike the ball with your instep (fig. 1c). Still keeping your eye on the ball, follow through to add power, aiming to hit through the centre of the ball (fig. 1d). Use your arms to keep your balance, and don't lift your head until the ball is on its way.

We have all seen players lofting the ball over the cross-bar, from what should have been an easy scoring position. The same thing will happen to you if you place the non-kicking foot too far behind the ball, causing the body to lean backwards at the moment of impact. On the other hand, if your non-kicking foot is placed too far in front of the ball, your shooting boot will tend to drive the ball into the ground.

Once you have mastered the most basic and important skill in soccer, you should be able to kick a ball correctly in all circumstances.

## Passing

The various passes and drives that make up a soccer player's armoury are merely different ways of propelling a football from one point to another. But the same rule applies as in the basic kicking technique – the ball won't go where you want it to unless your balance is right, and you position your feet correctly.

In the case of the **push pass**, for instance, the non-kicking foot is again placed alongside the ball, but not so close to it (fig. 2). Turn sideways on to the target player, and strike the ball with the inside of the other foot. Follow through smoothly, and keep your eye glued to the point of impact. Players who have perfected the push pass can send a ball gliding across the turf with tremendous accuracy – sometimes half the width of a full-size soccer pitch.

The **flick pass** is more difficult, and involves

flicking the ball forwards or sideways with the outside of the foot (fig. 3). Although lacking in power, it can be concealed until the last second, thus confusing an opponent as you move in one direction, and flick the ball in another.

The flick pass is not to be confused with **bending** the ball. As we know from televised football matches, the Latin-American players have turned this technique into a work of art. By cutting the foot across the inside, or the outside of the ball, they can make it 'bend' to right or left with incredible accuracy. But unless you are really skilled, and have mastered the 'banana' shot in training, never try to bend the ball at a crucial moment during a match ... or it might have disastrous consequences for your team!

The raw young player is well advised to restrict himself to the push pass and the **through pass,** as far as distributing the ball is concerned. Look for a team mate in an open space, and aim to deliver the ball to him with the clean, simple, straight-forward pass that is the essence of good football.

3

## Shooting and volleying

In the modern game, goals are scored with a wide variety of shots, drives, volleys, headers, scissors-kicks, etc. But concentrate on mastering the **low drive** first. Again, the position of the feet and the angle of the body are of vital importance. You will be on the move, of course, and the opportunity to shoot for goal may come right out of the blue, requiring a split-second reaction. But try to get that non-kicking foot alongside the ball, and your body leaning forward (fig. 4a). The knee of your kicking leg should be right over the ball as you make contact. (fig. 4b). Keep your toe down, and let fly with all the power you can muster. And notice how Cool Kevin is looking down at the ball. In fact, he will still be looking at it a split-second after he has kicked it!

The **volley** and the **half-volley** are much more difficult shots to perfect, and require endless hours of practice, especially the **overhead volley.** You will

find some training tips covering the more 'exotic' shots in football in Chapter 6. But don't worry too much if, at first, you find it difficult to master the volley. If you have real promise, you won't be over-looked by an astute soccer scout, just because you can't volley a football with the skill of Pele.

Even so, volleying is a vital ingredient of the game. During a match, a lot of balls will come to you above ground level. If you can 'lay them off' to a team mate, first time, without bringing the ball under control, then you have mastered one of the most difficult skills in soccer.

Apart from passing, you can use the volley to shoot for goal, and also to clear the ball from a packed penalty-area. Keep your eye on the ball, and try to get into the correct position before it arrives. At the moment of impact, you should be leaning away from the ball (fig. 5), with the arms thrown out to preserve balance. Hit the ball with your instep, not your toe.

5

Volleying at goal requires colossal timing, especially when the ball is coming at you about waist-high (fig. 6). Turn your body sideways to the flight of the ball, and swing your kicking leg almost horizontally, aiming to connect with the instep.

The **half-volley** – in which you kick the ball immediately after it bounces – is generally used for low drives and clearances. When shooting for goal, get the knee of your kicking leg over the ball, and point your toe downwards (fig. 7). If you do everything right, the ball should keep fairly low, and perhaps result in one of those spectacular goals that you only see in Match of the Day!

## Controlling the ball

If you try to trap an oncoming ball with a foot that is tense and rigid, the ball will rebound as if it has struck a plank. The same applies to every other part of the body which is used to receive and control the ball. In other words, you must learn the knack of relaxing the head, chest, or foot at the right moment, thus cushioning the ball and enabling you to bring it under control as quickly as possible.

## Ground passes

When receiving ground balls, be ready for unexpected bounces. Keeping the foot as close to the ground as possible, allow it to 'give' slightly on impact, thus absorbing the energy of the pass and 'killing' the ball.

If you can learn to control the ball, and turn with it, almost in the same movement, then your game is really making progress. Your non-kicking leg should be well anchored (fig. 8a) as you prepare to receive the ball. Start turning as you take the pace off the ball with a slightly angled foot (fig. 8b), so that the ball is still under control as you complete the turn (fig. 8c) and set off.

## Trapping

The art of bringing high balls or bouncing balls under instant control – as opposed to ground passes – is known as 'trapping'. Depending on the height and angle of the ball, the feet, the chest, and even the thigh can all be used to 'trap' lofted passes or rebounds. You can practise trapping the ball by yourself, with the help of a wall (fig. 9).

Again, it's vital to be relaxed at the point of impact, in order to kill the bounce. With the **sole trap**, for instance, cushion the ball delicately. Don't stamp, or jab at it, or you might do yourself – or the ball – an injury!

A dropping, slow-paced ball, which comes at you just below waist height, is best trapped with the thigh (fig. 10). But like the **chest trap** (fig. 11) it is a difficult skill for the young player to master. Think of your chest as a wall of bone and muscle. If you are not relaxed when a hard-driven shot smacks against that 'wall', the ball will rebound, hopelessly out of control.

9

Brazilian players have developed that instinctive knack of letting the whole of the upper body go limp, when taking a ball on the chest. They have learned to absorb the pace of the ball, so that it drops close to the feet, where it is easily brought under control.

But all the skill in the world won't turn you into a good player, if you just stand and wait for the ball. So *keep on your toes*, and stay alert. If an opponent beats you to the ball, you won't get the chance to show how well you can control it!

## Tackling

You don't have to be big and burly to be a good tackler. In our fast, modern game, defenders have to be quick off the mark. Speed, and an ability to 'read' the game are just as important as weight and strength. There are various types of tackles, and whichever one you use will be dictated by the flow of the game. Quite simply, to be a good tackler, you need determination and split-second timing. Never lunge in hopefully, or you will be 'left for dead', as they say. Wait until your opponent allows the ball to stray too far from his own feet, then dart in, using your toe to nudge the ball away from him, over the touchline, or to the feet of a team-mate.

The **front block tackle** (fig. 12) is a much more full-blooded business, and involves physical contact. But you've still got to time it right. You must aim to block or jam the ball against your opponent's feet or legs, thus forcing him off balance. Don't try to kick the ball away.

The **side block tackle** (fig. 13) is a kind of sliding tackle, in which the tackler hooks his foot around the ball and attempts to drag it away. Like the front block tackle, the intention is to retain possession of the ball, after you have made a successful tackle.

On the other hand, the straight-forward **sliding tackle** (fig. 14) is mainly used as a last resort. But it requires a lot of practice, and perfect timing. Many injuries in the local amateur game are caused by players, like Pushy Pete, who aren't really bothered if they get the man, or the ball. They're not deliberately vicious ... just clumsy. So practise the slide-tackle thoroughly before you attempt to use it in a match. Just one badly-timed slide-tackle in the penalty area, and you will probably give away a spot-kick, and lose a lot of friends!

## Dribbling

It goes without saying that you will never become a good dribbler until you have learned to control the ball properly. During the course of a dribble, you will be varying your pace, changing direction, feinting to right and left. But it's no good doing all that if you haven't got the ball!

The art of confusing an opponent with deceptive footwork and changes in acceleration, cannot really be taught. It can only be acquired through constant practice. You will find out for yourself that dribbling involves the use of the inside and outside of the foot, rather than the toe and instep. Watch the great players, the great wingmen. Notice how they check, and swerve, and accelerate. Sometimes, they will dawdle

with the ball, almost 'toying' with it, as they try to lure a defender into a rash and hasty tackle. Such skill comes naturally to the lucky ones, but the majority of us have to learn through endless practice.

Players like Pushy Pete will never learn how to dribble from looking at diagrams.

Diagrams don't allow for the fact that the ground may be wet, or sun-baked, or even frozen. Under such conditions, your sense of balance will be vital. So keep practising. Work hard on the dribbling routines that you will find in Chapter 6, and perhaps, in time, you will master the art of the body-swerve – that devastating sway of the hips which can bamboozle an opponent, when you are not even touching the ball.

## Heading

If you are wary about heading a football, then you are in good company. Some of our better-known professionals will only head a football as a last resort. But there is nothing to be frightened of, as long as you do it correctly.

Use a softer ball at first, to build up your confidence. Practise keeping the ball in the air with your head (fig. 15a).

15a

15b

Keep your eyes wide open, and strike the ball with the centre of your forehead (fig. 15b). As your confidence grows, you can practise heading on the move, by throwing the ball against a wall, and following up to head the rebound (fig. 16). Once you have got the 'feel' of heading a ball, and conquered the temptation to close your eyes, you can start thinking about power and distance.

To gain power, and to avoid hurting yourself, you must learn to lock your neck muscles when making contact with the ball. Swing your body back from the waist (fig. 17, overleaf), and ram the ball with your forehead, punching it forwards and downwards.

Under match conditions, never wait for the

16

**17**

ball to come to you, even though you may have plenty of time and room. The player who is on the move will gain added height and power.

When jumping to head a ball, you should be a fraction higher than the ball before contact (fig. 18). The head, neck and shoulders should all combine in the whip-lashing motion that results in a really powerful header (fig. 19).

At first, young players will find it difficult to time a leaping header correctly. Ideally, you should

**18**

strive to be airborne a fraction of a second before the ball arrives. This is particularly important in the case of the flicked header, which is used to pass the ball to a teammate, as opposed to clearances and goal-scoring attempts.

But like all the basic skills we have dealt with, the ability to head a football correctly can only be achieved through constant practice. Devote every spare moment to improving your ball control. Practise kicking, heading, dribbling and passing. Anything, in fact, which will improve your skills.

It must be obvious, even to Pushy Pete, that the better you are at football, the more you will enjoy it.

# 3  PLAYERS AND POSITIONS

Mastering some of the basic skills of soccer is one thing. The problem of choosing a position in which you can make the best use of those skills is quite another.

Most soccer enthusiasts will already know that football is an eleven-a-side game, played on a rectangular pitch, with a round thing called a ball. Each team of eleven players is composed of a Goalkeeper, Defenders, Midfield players and Forwards. It's when we start talking about these various positions in terms of the modern game, that it all becomes a little complicated.

We have all heard panels of experts discussing the merits of Left-Sided Back Four players, Sweepers and Centre-Backs. Forwards are not just 'forwards' any more. They are Front Runners, Target-Men, Link-Men, and Strikers. Such terms are the 'jargon' of football, and it will increase your understanding of the modern game if you become familiar with them. But the beginner who tries to slot himself into one of these positions without expert advice, could be wasting his time and energy. It's best to wait until you are playing regularly for a particular team, under a manager who knows his business.

If you play football regularly, you will soon begin to build up a picture of your strengths, and weaknesses. Perhaps you are the best dribbler in the team, but your shooting is abysmal. Or perhaps your lack of ball control prevents you from exploiting your cannonball shot. Then again, you might relish the challenge of a fierce tackle, or discover that you feel more at home in goal. But try to keep an open mind about where you should play. The most important thing to remember, is that players are expected to be much more versatile than they used to be. The days are long gone when a winger, for example, remained glued to the touchline in his opponents' half, waiting for a pass, so that he could set off on a dazzling solo dribble.

With the exception of the goalkeeper, the modern player must be prepared to support his colleagues, whether attacking or defending. He must 'put himself about', as they say. In the course of a match, you will see forwards falling back to help their defenders to clear a corner-kick or a free-kick. Defenders move up confidently to assist in an attack, knowing that a team-mate will be covering the gap they have left. In other words, the modern player must be fit enough to cover every zone of the pitch. He must think in terms of attack and defence – the broad, total sweep of the game. He must aim for all-round ability.

But modern football is also about specialists. Particular players are required to play specific roles within a team's overall tactics. So let's look at the basic roles – or positions – in detail.

## Goalkeeper

The unique skills of the Goalkeeper are discussed in Chapter 4. The young player with agility and a safe pair of hands, who wants to follow in the footsteps of Phil Parkes, will have no need to ask, 'Where should I play?'

## Defenders

To be a good Defender, you will need to be fairly tall, physically strong, and willing to tackle fearlessly. This doesn't mean that you should forget about defensive play just because you are small and light. But it's obvious that a player with height and strength is better equipped to cope with those long, dangerous crosses into the goalmouth. He should be able to clear them with a well-timed leap, and a powerful header.

The ideal defender will also have a keen positional sense – an ability to anticipate the direction of a pass, and destroy an attack with a timely interception. He will strive to keep himself between his own goal and the player he is supposed to be marking. And he will not allow himself to be caught 'ball-watching'. This means that he will not make the mistake of devoting his whole attention to the ball, while his opponent sneaks into an open space behind his back. At the same time, he will guard against being lured out of position by an opposing forward. You will only look silly following an opponent around the pitch, shadowing him like a hawk, while someone else is hammering the ball into your net!

An intelligent defender will weigh up the priorities in a flash, and position himself accordingly.

And finally, if you are going to succeed as a defender, you will need a good turn of speed. You must be able to move up quickly in support of an attack, and retreat just as swiftly to get behind the ball, when your own team comes under pressure.

## Midfield players

Midfield players are sometimes referred to as 'linkmen', because they provide a link between attackers and defenders. Consequently, they must be exceptionally fit. They must have the stamina to collect a clearance from a defender, make ground, and supply an accurate pass, and then be on hand to take part in the final movements of the attack.

It is in midfield where possession of the ball is won and lost, and the outcome of many matches decided. It is also the area where the roles of various players often overlap. One team might use a formation

in which **deep-lying forwards** are expected to chase back and win the ball from a rival midfield man, whereas their opponents might employ two or more players to 'police' the middle of the park. In each case, we are seeing 'link-men' in operation – players whose job it is to provide the springboard for a continuous, aggressive assault on the opposing goal. Franz Beckenbauer, the former West German international, is perhaps the best example of a 'pure' midfield player, whereas Colin Bell of Manchester City played some of his best games for England as a deep-lying forward.

So if you feel that you would like to be involved in every phase of the game – in the 'engine room' of soccer – then it's likely that the best position for you is midfield.

But remember that you will be expected to work harder than any other player in the team!

## Forwards

In these days of complicated tactical formations, it is sometimes difficult to distinguish forwards from defenders ... especially when the experts get going. An old-fashioned forward line consisted of five players (two wingers, two inside-forwards, and a centre-forward) who rarely strayed from the positions in which they started the game. But when the modern soccer coach mentions forward play, he is probably thinking in terms of **central strikers** and **wingers,** as opposed to deep-lying forwards, who also function as ball-winners.

The main function of the **central striker** is, quite simply, to score goals. Managers will gladly spend a small fortune on players who can hit the back of the net with machine-like regularity.

But to join the ranks of these soccer supermen, you will need, first and foremost, to be able to shoot hard and accurately with both feet. You will need explosive speed to get past those quick-tackling defenders, and convert half-chances into goals. You will have to master the art of 'screening' the ball from defenders, holding it tightly under control while team-mates run into scoring positions.

The ideal central striker will combine the goal-poaching qualities of Jimmy Greaves with the finishing power of Argentina's Mario Kempes. He will be able to strike for goal with glancing, and bullet-like headers, even when under tremendous pressure. In the modern game of packed, tight-marking defences, the central striker has to be big, and strong enough to battle for every inch of space, and make the best possible use of it. He must be willing to make a 'target man' of himself, unselfishly making space for his colleagues. It's not surprising, is it, that there's a serious shortage of good central strikers?

There is also a shortage of **wing forwards.** Genuine wingers almost vanished from the game, because many managers placed their faith in the 'work-horse' type of player. But now the winger is finding favour again. He is recognised as a forward who can add 'width' to a team's tactics – a player who can create openings for his colleagues with his speed and dribbling skills. To some extent, the role of the

winger hasn't changed very much. When the ball is in his own half, he is still required to roam the touchline, so that the midfield men know instinctively where to find him. If you have a flair for dribbling, and can 'chip' or cross the ball accurately to team-mates in the goalmouth, then you might develop into a useful winger ... particularly if you are lightly-built. Wing forwards, playing wide down the touchline, are rarely involved in such a bruising battle for the ball as the central strikers. They can use their speed to cut inside, looking for the chance to pounce on to a cross from the opposite wing, and score a vital goal with an accurate shot or header.

By now, you should have a general understanding of the various positions and the special abilities that are needed to fill them. But if you are still confused about where you should play, don't let it worry you. Subtle changes in the tactics of football are taking place all the time, and the young player would be well advised to 'feel' his way into the game.

For instance, if you are rotten at dribbling but possess a powerful kick, you may decide that you are best fitted to be a defender. But what happens, a year or two later, after you have improved your dribbling with practice, and you *still* possess a powerful shot? The chances are you will start thinking about scoring goals ... as a forward!

So listen to your teachers, and your coaches. Let them channel your developing skills into the position that suits you best.

And when you go to a professional football match, remember that many of the players you are watching – forwards, defenders, and midfield men – probably began their careers by playing in a completely different position.

# 4 BETWEEN THE STICKS

Not every professional goalkeeper is as tall and well-balanced as Phil Parkes, or as powerfully-built as Peter Shilton, of Nottingham Forest. Some of them are thin and rakish, and others are comparatively small, like Paul Cooper, who made such a valuable contribution to Ipswich Town's victory over Arsenal

in the 1977–78 F.A. Cup Final.

So if the idea of playing in goal appeals to you, don't be put off by the fact that you are not as tall and as solid as an oak tree. If you have reasonable agility, and a safe pair of hands, there is every chance that you might develop into an efficient goalkeeper.

But you must be fit! A fit and supple body means an alert mind and a keen eye – qualities which are needed to make those 'reflex' saves that the football commentators are always talking about.

Pushy Pete could never make a reflex save, because he's overweight.

Perhaps nobody told him that a few simple daily exercises will help to build up the suppleness and agility which form the basis of the goalkeeper's special skills. But first, let's examine those skills in detail.

## Catching

During the course of a football match, a goalkeeper must expect to be bombarded with a wide range of shots and crosses, coming at him from varying heights and angles. But wherever possible, you should aim to get your body behind the line of flight of the ball.

In the case of a chest-high shot (fig. 1), the hands and arms must 'swallow' the ball. As you grasp it tightly to your chest, lean slightly forward to maintain balance, and absorb the power of the shot.

Shots coming straight at you along the ground may look easier to handle, but deal with them firmly. Keep your eyes on the ball, and watch for any unexpected bounces and deflections. And keep your legs together (fig. 2). Your legs are your last line of defence if you should happen to fumble the ball, and allow it to

3

**2**

squeeze through your hands.

With high shots and crosses, a goalkeeper can really demonstrate that he is in control of his area. Instead of waiting for the ball, go out and meet it. Catch it with a well-timed jump, keeping your thumbs as close to each other as possible (fig. 3). As soon as contact has been made, pull the ball down, and cuddle it into your chest.

## Deflections and punching

One of the golden rules of goalkeeping is 'safety first'. So never punch or deflect an incoming ball, if you can catch it safely. A wild punch which fails to connect can put your defence in all sorts of trouble.

But if you have decided to punch the ball clear, because the ball is coming at you too fast, or too high – or because you are under severe pressure from opposing players – then punch it away as hard as you can, back in the direction from which it came. If possible, use both clenched fists, held close together, and aim for the centre of the ball (fig. 4).

As with punching, you should only deflect the ball when you are certain that it would be too dangerous to attempt a catch. Use the palm of the hand to push the ball over the cross-bar (fig. 5). But push the ball firmly. Make sure that it doesn't hit the crossbar, and rebound back into play ... straight to the feet of an opponent!

## Diving

There are few sights in football more exciting than a spectacular diving save. But a jack-knifing leap, fingers stretching to tip the ball over the bar or around an upright, is the sensible goalkeeper's last resort. It is far better to catch the ball, if you can, and spark off an attack with an accurate kick or throw.

If, however, you have no alternative but to dive for the ball, its your split-second sense of anticipation which will mean the difference between a fine save and a goal. But you don't need the facilities of a First Division club to devise some simple training rountines, which will help to sharpen your reactions.

1 Position yourself about ten metres from the angle of a wall, and kick a football against it. As the ball rebounds at an unexpected angle, attempt to cut it off before it passes you, by diving to the right or left.
2 For this exercise, you'll need the help of a friend. Stand with your back to the wall, and as he shoots the ball past you, see how quickly you can turn and dive for the rebound.
3 This time you don't need the wall. Stand with your back to your partner, and about fifteen metres away from him. As he shoots, he lets out a shout – the signal for you to turn and dive quickly enough to intercept the shot.

4 Using two balls, your partner kicks or rolls the first ball to your (the goalkeeper's) right, and the second ball to your left. If you can save the first ball, pick yourself up, and dive in the opposite direction in time to stop the second, then your reactions are really speeding up.

But whether diving for high balls or ground balls, remember that you are going to hit the ground with a pretty hard thud. So choose a patch of soft earth for practice sessions or, better still, borrow an old mattress. In time, you will learn how to fall correctly, and develop the confidence to try out the exercises on hard ground.

## Ground saves

Diving for ground shots requires courage and timing, especially when an opponent is coming in hard behind the ball. Resist the temptation to throw yourself head-first at the ball. Allow the body to fall sideways (fig. 6), using your knee and thigh to cushion the impact with the ground, and hug the ball into your chest.

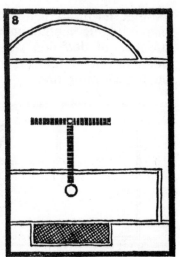

This also applies to the more spectacular business of diving at the feet of an opponent who has broken clean through the defence. As you dive to smother the ball, roll towards him, thus protecting the ball with your shoulder and forearm (fig. 7). As always, clutch the ball tightly, and pull it into your chest as quickly as possible.

## Positioning

The ability to position yourself correctly is almost as important as having a safe pair of hands.

Just think about it for a moment. A goalkeeper spends most of the game looking towards the opposite end of the pitch. His own goal is behind him, out of his field of vision.

But there's no need to keep looking over your shoulder, and risk taking your eye off the ball at a crucial moment. Phil Parkes works off an imaginary 'T' shape, with the 'crossbar' of the T running through the penalty-spot (fig. 8). In moments of crisis he knows exactly where he is in relation to the goal, without having to glance behind him. Once you have mastered this 'mental geography', you'll find that the problem of deciding whether to stay between the posts or run out to meet an incoming ball won't seem such a daunting one.

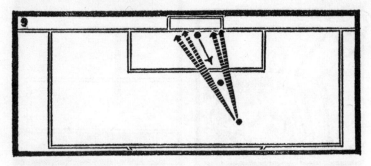

**Narrowing the angle**  In the case of an opponent who is coming at you unchallenged, you *must* run out at him, thereby reducing the area of the goal at which he can aim (fig. 9, position 2). If your timing is right, and you have positioned yourself correctly, he will have to shoot from farther out or attempt a lob. In each case, a finger-tip will be all that's needed to deflect the ball wide of the goal.

But whether you are coming out to challenge an opponent, or waiting on the goal-line for a corner, be decisive! A sound positional sense will only be gained through experience, and by watching top-class goalkeepers at work. Notice how commanding they are. Even during televised football matches, you can see them shouting and gesticulating: telling their team-mates where to position themselves.

Shout loudly, and with authority. And once you have made a decision, stick to it. There is nothing more inspiring to hard-pressed defenders than a goalkeeper who rules the roost in his own penalty-area – a goalkeeper they can rely on.

## Physical fitness

A safe pair of hands, sound positional sense, courage and timing – all these vital goalkeeping skills will be diminished if you are not physically fit.

The best goalkeepers have strong arms, strong legs, and a strong stomach. But there's no need to rush out and enrol for a body-building course, designed to turn you into a Mr Universe. All you need to strengthen your legs, for instance, is the staircase in your own home.

This exercise is called 'step-ups'. Simply place your right, or left foot on the first tread of the stairs, and bring the other foot up to join it. Then step down again, one foot at a time, and repeat the process ... say, about a dozen times.

Building up the stomach muscles requires a little more effort. Lie on your back with the back of your head and the palms of your hands touching the ground. Lift your legs, held close together, to an angle of 45 degrees. Hold them there while you count to seven, then slowly lower.

For strengthening the arms, there's nothing like a good, old-fashioned 'press-up'. Start with five press-ups in your first exercise session, adding an extra press-up each day, until you can perform ten in a row. Relax for a second or two between press-ups.

There's no need to exhaust yourself. Just five minutes' exercise per day will gradually build up your strength and stamina. But have a chat with your parents first, or the P.E. tutor at school. Make sure that your training programme – however brief – is adjusted to your present standard of health and fitness. Otherwise, you might find yourself standing on the touchline with a pulled muscle, while someone else takes your place between the sticks!

# 5 TALKING ABOUT TACTICS

It's not really accurate to say that football is a simple game – not these days, anyway. Very basically, a football match can be described as a game in which the players of each side seek to retain possession of the ball by passing it accurately to one another, until an opportunity arrives to force the ball into the opposing net. But such a simple definition cannot hope to convey an idea of the complex thrust and counter-thrust of the modern professional game – the bewildering, inter-weaving patterns of attack and defence.

Most of the goals that you see scored by professional teams on a Saturday afternoon are probably the result of an intricate team-plan which was worked out long before the kick-off.

A team-plan is based on certain tactics ... tactics which may vary enormously from those used by the opposition. One of the main functions of a club manager is to assess the strengths and weaknesses of the opposing team, and plan his own team's tactics accordingly. If his tactics do not work, he will change them, right in the middle of a game; perhaps re-shuffling his players into an attacking formation instead of a defensive one, or signalling his strikers to drop back when his team comes under heavy pressure. This is why football, at its best, can be such an exciting and flowing spectacle – a rivetting tactical struggle, with each side striving to take a grip on the game.

When you consider the number of different ways in which eleven players can be positioned and deployed, it's surprising that the old-fashioned formation of 2–3–5 (two full-backs, three half-backs, and five forwards) dominated British and European football for so long. It wasn't until the 'Magic Magyars' of

Hungary trounced England 6–3 at Wembley Stadium in 1953, that the average soccer fan (and quite a few managers) realised that there was more to football than 2–3–5. The days when six members of a football team spent most of the time guarding their own goal were clearly numbered. The game was becoming more 'fluid', and the specialist team formations that we know today were beginning to evolve.

## 4–2–4

The young player who is keen to explore the intricacies of football strategy will find it easiest to experiment with the 4–2–4 formation (fig. 1). Starting from the back (the goalkeeper is not included, because his position never changes), this formation consists of 4 defenders, 2 midfield players and 4 strikers. It is a fairly balanced formation, with an equal emphasis on attack and defence . . . which means that the players will not necessarily restrict themselves to the positions shown in the diagram. The four front-runners will be constantly changing position to try to confuse opposing defenders, whereas the four defenders will rarely play in a straight line across the pitch. There is always the danger of being 'caught square', by the

1
Outside Left     Twin Centre Forward — Strikers     Outside Right

Link-men

Left Back     Twin Centre Half     Right Back

Goalkeeper

sudden, through pass that beats the whole lot of them. As we have seen from the chapter on positional play, the defenders will be constantly covering each other, and looking for the chance to make a sudden sprint upfield and become a temporary winger. Similarly, the two midfield men must be ever-ready to join in an attack, or help out the defence. They must provide the link which ensures an exciting, continuous flow of attacking football.

## 4–3–3

This is the formation that Sir Alf Ramsey used when England won the World Cup in 1966. As you will see from the diagram (fig. 2), an extra midfield man is included in place of one of the strikers. Players using a 4–3–3 formation must be at a peak of physical fitness, because every man – with the exception of the goalkeeper – is expected to run himself into the ground in support of his colleagues. Ramsey dispensed with orthodox wingers, which is why we saw full-backs like Cohen and Wilson, galloping up the touchline, and crossing the ball into the opposing goalmouth.

It's doubtful if a brilliant individualist could survive in a 4–3–3 formation, unless he is prepared to sacrifice

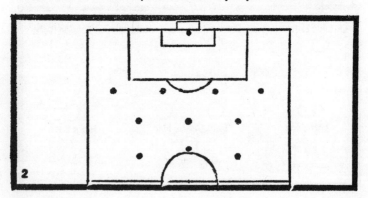

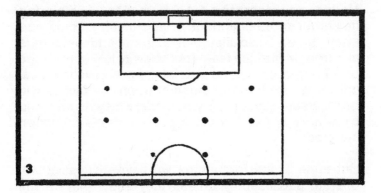

some of his natural flair, and do his share of the running and foraging that 4-3-3 demands. When this formation first appeared, many football fans were utterly bewildered by it. The young player will be equally bewildered if he does not fully understand the purpose of 4-3-3. It only worked successfully for England because every player in the team had a chance to master the mysteries of 4-3-3 through regular training sessions, held over several weeks.

## 4-4-2

If you support a club that plays exciting, attacking football which produces lots of goals, then it's safe to say that your favourite team does *not* employ a 4-4-2 formation (fig. 3). As the diagram shows, nine players, including the goalkeeper, are used in defence-minded roles. A manager may be forced to use 4-4-2 because he hasn't got enough good strikers in his squad to adopt a 4-2-4 formation. He may be compelled to field a team capable of winning absolute mastery in midfield, so that one of his front-runners can snatch a vital, winning goal.

Such dull, negative tactics are often dictated by a sheer lack of goal-scoring talent. But even exciting, attacking teams such as Manchester United and Real

Madrid, may resort to a 4–4–2 formation when playing in European competitions which involve home and away 'legs'. Specialist ball-winners and defenders are brought into the team for the away leg, in the hope of forcing a draw, and establishing a psychological advantage for the home game, when the tactics will be reversed. One or more defenders may be replaced by attackers, and the more positive 4–2–4 formation adopted.

But none of the formations we have discussed will operate successfully unless they allow players the freedom to make their own split-second decisions in a particular situation. You can't expect your opponents to stand by while your beautiful team-plan results in an avalanche of goals. They will do their best to counteract it. And they may do it so successfully that your manager will have to change his tactics to avoid losing control of the game.

Injuries can also force a manager to change his style of play. For example, an attacking 4–2–4 formation may have to be abandoned if one of his strikers is injured, and the substitute is a defender. And what if both teams decide to employ identical defensive formations? The result will be a boring, negative game, producing snores instead of cheers.

Formations, then, are merely broad outlines of defensive or attacking play, which may be subtly changed or modified according to the state of the game. A wide variety of tactical moves and 'set-pieces' can take place within an overall team-plan. And rather than confuse himself by trying to master the theory behind the various formations, the young player should concentrate on practising the individual moves and techniques that make the formations work.

## Small-sided games

The best way to start 'reading' and analysing the tactics of football, is to organise some six-a-side, or even three-a-side games with your friends. But mark out a smaller pitch, say, about a third of the size of a normal one. It's much easier to try out some simple tactics, and actually see them working, if you limit the size of the playing area.

Start with some simple passing movements, mixing short passes with long passes. See how many passes you can string together before the other side gains possession of the ball.

Practise **screening** the ball (fig. 4). Use your body as a shield to prevent an opponent from getting at the ball, while your team-mates run into open spaces. Try to anticipate the movements of your team-mates and support them. When you want the ball, make sure that you are in the best position to receive it. Call for it loudly and commandingly. Slowly but surely, you will begin to appreciate the meaning of team-work. You will begin to sense how a football match can be broken down into passing confrontations between small groups of players. Without unselfish team-work, and accurate passing, even the most carefully-planned tactics are doomed to failure.

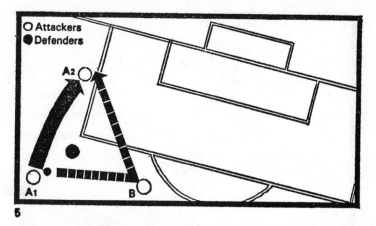

O Attackers
● Defenders

A2

A1    B

5

## The wall pass

As its name suggests, the wall pass grew out of
street matches and playground kick-abouts. Most of
us have by-passed an opponent by flicking a tennis-
ball against a wall, or a fence, and darting around him
to snap up the rebound. On the field of play, in a two-
against-one situation, a team-mate becomes the
'wall'. As you flick the ball to him, and dart past an
opponent, he should return the ball smartly, at an
angle, as if the ball has 'bounced' off him (fig. 5).

But the wall pass is not as simple as it sounds. As
you bring the ball up to a defender, you should be
trying to take various factors into account. Are you
moving at the right speed? How close can you take
the ball to the defender before parting with it? If you
part with the ball too soon, he may have time to turn
and prevent your colleague from making the return
pass. And is your team-mate in the right position?
Is he far enough away from the defender to have time
to complete the wall pass? Or should you forget the
whole thing, because you haven't got a computer for
a brain! A player like Pushy Pete would probably need
a computer to work it all out!

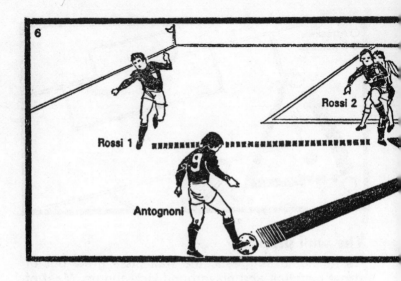

Seriously, the wall pass is a valuable exercise in simple tactics, because it helps you to develop the habit of reading the game ... especially when a second defender is in the vicinity. You will have to note the positions of defenders and team-mates in a split-second, and then decide if a wall pass is 'on'.

Consider the brilliant goal scored by Italy's Bettega against Argentina in the 1978 World Cup (fig. 6). Although Bettega and his team-mate, Rossi, were both closely marked, they must have realised in a flash that the Argentinian defenders were positioned in such a way that they were vulnerable to a wall pass.

As you can see from the diagram, Antognoni passed the ball to Bettega, who promptly flicked it to Rossi. Acting as the 'wall', Rossi returned the ball into Bettega's path as he darted around his marker, and scored the goal which beat Argentina – their only defeat in the World Cup.

But the goal could not have been scored if Rossi

Bettega 3

Bettega 2

Bettega 1

had not been in the right position, which is a valuable lesson in 'running off the ball'. Even when you are not in possession of the ball, you should be alive to what is going on around you. Are you in a good position to receive a pass if a colleague comes under pressure? Are you watching the movements of opposing players, in case they mount a sudden attack? In short, are you involving yourself in the problems of your colleagues, and working as hard as possible for your team?

Bettega's goal was brilliantly taken, but it was born out of the unselfish support of his colleague and a simple tactic called a wall pass.

## Set pieces

Throws-in, corner-kicks, free kicks, and penalty kicks – in the modern game, these are all known as 'set pieces'. When you see a goal scored from a set-piece, it's probably the result of hours of practice and experiment in training-sessions. So let's see how they fit into the general tactics of a football match.

## Throw-in

Before we discuss how a throw-in may be used as a form of attack, let's make sure that you know how to execute a throw-in properly, within the Laws of the game. The thrower must face the field of play, and the ball must be held in both hands, and thrown from behind and over the head (fig. 7). Part of each foot must be on, or outside the touchline. Bend the knees slightly, and hold the ball with your fingers spread out, with the thumbs at the back of the ball. Take a short run-up to the line if you wish, but remember the the power of the throw-in comes from a whip-lashing motion of the body, followed by a windmill-like follow-through of the arms. With a little dedicated practice, you will discover that the ball can be thrown quite considerable distances.

7

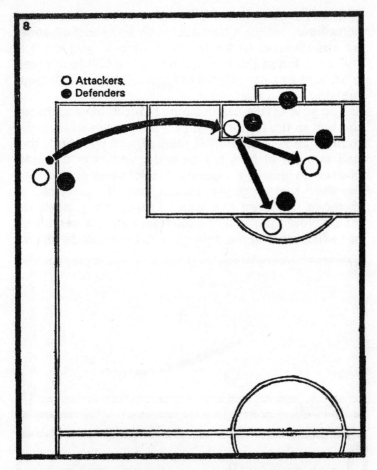

8.

○ Attackers
● Defenders

Expert professionals can reach the goalmouth from the touchline with a long throw-in. Such a throw can cause all sorts of problems for the defence, especially if the attacking side includes a couple of tall strikers, who can hustle the goalkeeper and get in a glancing header to the feet of a colleague (fig. 8).

You can work out a simple but effective tactic with a couple of your team-mates. Let's call them A and B (fig. 9). As you shape as if to throw the ball to A, he runs back, taking a defender with him, and creating an open space. At the last split-second, you change the direction of the throw, lobbing the ball to the feet of B, who has darted into the gap left by the defender marking A.

The golden rule, when taking a throw-in, is to throw the ball to the left or right of a team-mate or into his path as he sets off. If he is marked, and you throw the ball straight at him, the defender will have a better chance to get in a decisive tackle. And always remember that a player cannot be off-side from a throw-in. So even if a winger runs into a position which would normally be off-side, you can send him speeding clear of the defence with an accurate throw.

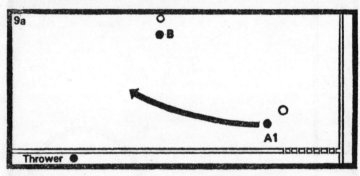

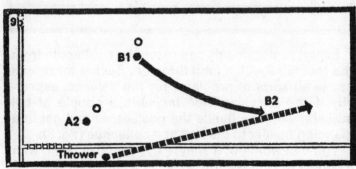

## Corner kick

Most young players will have to practise long and
hard to master the two main types of corner-kick,
the **in-swinger** and the **out-swinger** (fig. 10). The
ability to make the ball swing away from the goal or
towards the goal, is an art in itself. But if you are a

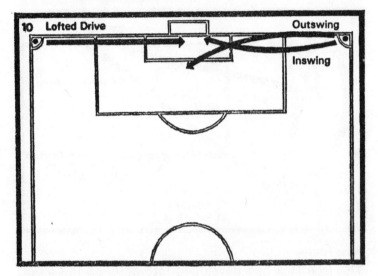

10    Lofted Drive                                    Outswing

Inswing

strong and accurate kicker, and you have spotted that
the opposing goalkeeper is unhappy with high balls,
you can cause a lot of problems by simply lofting the
ball into your opponents' goal-mouth.

Young players may find it more profitable to experiment with the **short corner.** The purpose of the short
corner is to draw defenders out of the goal area. In
the diagram overleaf you can see how player A has
played a short corner to B, luring defenders C and D
out of position. 'A' darts into a position which will
give him more room to unleash an accurate cross, or
lay off the ball to a midfield man who has moved up
to join the attack. Of course, the tactic will fail if your

passing is inaccurate, so get together with your friends and practise some short corner set-pieces. Include a wall pass if you like. The short corner can be used with devastating effect, and is an ideal tactic for teams whose forwards are small and lightly-built.

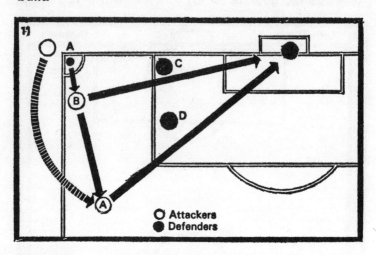

O Attackers
● Defenders

## Free kicks

The free kick has developed into perhaps the most exciting and carefully-planned set piece in the modern game. There are two types of free kick, direct and indirect. If awarded an **indirect free kick**, the ball must be touched by a second player before a goal can be scored, whereas you can score from a **direct free kick** without another player touching the ball.

When a direct free kick is awarded to an attacking team near the defenders' penalty-area, a number of defenders usually form a 'wall', to prevent a direct shot being made at goal. To counteract this, the modern professional is encouraged to practise the technique of making the ball 'bend' around, or over

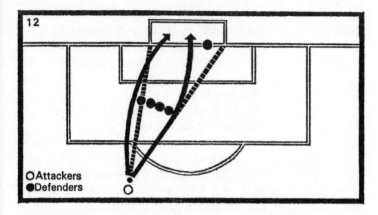

## 12

O Attackers
● Defenders

the defensive wall, in order to score (fig. 12). But if you haven't yet mastered the art of the banana shot, it is best to concentrate on tactics which are designed to create space for an angled shot at goal (fig. 13). This applies to both direct and indirect free kicks.

Even junior school teams can achieve surprising results by practising free kick set-pieces during training sessions. With the help of your teacher or

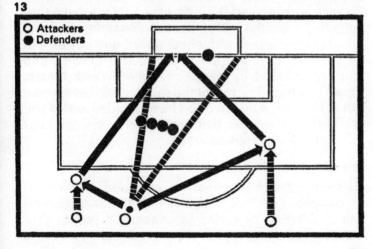

13

O Attackers
● Defenders

coach, certain players can be detailed to act as decoys, making 'dummy' runs as you shape to take the kick. Hopefully, they will draw defenders out of position, creating space for a colleague on the opposite side of the wall. Alternatively, as the defenders pause uncertainly, confused by your darting, crisscrossing team mates, a gap might appear in the wall, enabling you to get in a snap shot at goal.
the diagram overleaf you can see how player A has
So don't waste your free kicks. In games which are dominated by equally-matched defences, they can often produce that vital goal which means the difference between victory and a goal-less draw.

**Penalties**

There are no hard and fast rules about taking penalty kicks. If you can hit a ball low, hard and accurately, just inside one of the uprights, then no goalkeeper on earth will be able to stop it ... unless he is blessed with superhuman powers of anticipation!

With one of your friends acting as goalkeeper, practise penalty shots whenever you get the chance. Players with powerful shots may achieve better results by hitting the ball as hard as possible, aiming to beat the goalkeeper with sheer speed and power. But be positive. If your team is awarded a penalty, and you are detailed to take it ... take a deep breath. Then another. Try to compose yourself before you run at the ball. And once you have decided where you are going to aim the ball, never, *never* change your mind at the last split-second.

## Goalkeeper

Although the goalkeeper is excluded from team formations, this does not mean that he has no tactical value as far as attacking is concerned. When professional goalkeepers make a save, or cut off a centre, they don't just boot the ball blindly back up the pitch. With a quick throw or an accurate clearance to a team-mate, they can spark off a move which brings the opposing team under immediate pressure. This is known as 'distribution' – the manner in which a goalkeeper disposes of the ball after he has caught it. Some goalkeepers can throw the ball colossal distances ... but the beginner should concentrate on accuracy first. Power and distance will come as you gain experience.

In the case of the **long throw** try to imagine that you are throwing a javelin (fig. 14). The power comes from the shoulders, with a flick of the wrist at the

14

moment of release, followed by a strong follow-through.

The short, **underarm throw** (fig. 15) can be made with greater accuracy, but it should only be used when rolling the ball to team mates who are positioned just outside your penalty-area. Again, a good follow-through is essential But *never* throw the ball to a heavily-marked colleague. If you cannot spot a

well-placed team mate, kick the ball clear as hard and accurately as you can. And if you can do it while opposing players are still swarming around your goalmouth, so much the better.

## Tactics and the beginner

Although many of the basic moves and set-pieces we have discussed can be used quite effectively in junior matches, it should always be remembered that managers and coaches are constantly experimenting with the tactics of modern football. New theories and formations are emerging all the time. In the opinion of many experts, the young player should concentrate on improving his football skills, and forget about tactics.

Perhaps they are right. Even professional players, moving from one club to another, may have to change their style of play to suit the particular tactics that their new manager employs. At the same time, the young player who has made some effort to understand the complexities of the modern game will be of greater value to his team.

So the next time you go to a professional football match, don't spend most of your time chanting, and jeering the opposition. Concentrate on one player. See if you can analyse the particular job of work that he is doing for his team, down there on the pitch. Is he being used as a solitary spear-head, or is he playing a purely defensive game? Watch for subtle changes in his tactical role, following an injury to a team mate, or as a result of instructions received from his team 'bench'.

Whether you are watching, playing or practising, get into the habit of 'reading' the game and you just might surprise your teacher or coach with the extent of your knowledge of football!

# 6 BE YOUR OWN COACH

'That lad is going to be a great footballer one day. He's a natural!' It's an old saying in football, but not necessarily a wise one. Some players are, of course, fortunate enough to be born with a natural flair for their chosen sport – a kind of instinctive skill. Such early promise might be enough to send your Dad into raptures of pride and admiration.

But unless your Dad happens to be an experienced soccer scout, he may not realise that even Osvaldo Ardiles needed expert coaching, and regular, dedicated practice to develop into the great player that he is.

Some of you may attend schools or youth clubs which organise special coaching sessions. Or perhaps you live near a professional football club which holds 'open days'. If so, go along. Mix with the professionals, and train with them, if the opportunity arises. Devour every piece of advice that is offered to you.

But if you live in an area where the coaching facilities are almost non-existent, don't be too discouraged. The player who is prepared to work hard at improving and sharpening his skills stands the best chance of success, and there are plenty of simple practices and training routines which require the presence of only one person – yourself.

## Touch

Many managers and coaches talk about a player's 'touch' on the ball. But what on earth is touch? Quite simply, it is a measurement of your ability to make a football do exactly what you want it to do, particularly when controlling the ball. The quicker you can bring a ball under control, the more time you will have to decide what you are going to do with it. A player with good touch is deciding when and where he is going to pass the ball, even as it reaches him. He is looking ahead. He is developing 'vision', the hallmark of all the great players. So your touch on the ball is vital.

Test your sense of touch with a tennis ball to begin with (fig. 1). Lift it with either foot, and

you have progressed to a full-size ball. Vary the exercise by using the inside of your foot (fig. 2). Tap the ball from one foot to the other, slowly at first, then speeding up, varying your rhythm all the time. Sometimes, because your touch on the ball is too hard or too soft, you will lose control of it, and it will bounce away from you. But gradually, the more you practise, the more your feet will become attuned to the ball. You are getting the 'feel' of a

let it bounce. Catch the ball with your instep, and let it bounce again. Keep the sequence going as long as you can. As your confidence grows, start using larger balls, until football at the end of your legs!

Set yourself little targets. If your 'wrong' foot is your left foot, make a vow that you won't go in to watch your favourite television programme until you have flicked or tapped the ball up in the air, six times in a row, with your left foot. A week later, increase your target to ten in a row. But wait until you are certain that you can do six. A good sense of touch doesn't come easily.

## Dribbling

Of all the soccer skills that you can practise on your own, dribbling is perhaps the most enjoyable, and the most rewarding for the young player. All you need is a line of obstacles (large stones, bottles, cricket stumps) with gaps of about two metres between them.

Slowly and carefully at first, start weaving through the line of obstacles with the ball. Move left of the first obstacle, then to the right, and so on (fig. 3). Use the inside and the outside of your foot, keeping the ball tightly under control. Try not to disturb or knock down the obstacles. As your touch improves, gradually build up the speed of your runs. Move up the line using only one foot to guide the ball, changing to the other foot on the way back.

This is an excellent exercise for sharpening control with your weaker foot. The young player who admits that he is hopeless with his left foot or his right foot, and does nothing about it, will never be more than just an average footballer. So avoid the temptation to use your best foot all the time. Concentrate on dribbling with your weaker foot. As you sharpen your touch and control, you will find your balance improving as well – your ability to wriggle out of the tight situations that you will encounter in a match. Teaching yourself to become a two-footed player requires long hours of hard practice, but it will

all seem worthwhile on the day that you score a goal, or beat an opponent, with your 'wrong peg'. It's a tremendous feeling!

## Two-footed control

You don't need obstacles for this exercise. Just mark out a straight line on the ground. Chalk it or paint it, or simply make a dead-straight groove in the earth with a stick.

Move along the line with the ball, tapping the ball from one foot to the other (fig. 4). Vary your speed. Nurse the ball along, imagining defenders popping up in front of you. Make sudden darts and swerves shaping to go one way, then checking at the last second to push the ball in the other direction. Almost without realising it, you are teaching yourself the technique of the 'feint' (fig. 5). The ability to un-balance and beat an opponent with a well-timed feint cannot be learned overnight. But the straight-line practice is useful for building up your confidence and skill, before you try out a dribbling feint on your friends or in a match.

## Wall practices

There are numerous ways of improving your skill with the help of a wall or a solid fence, as long as you

don't make a nuisance of yourself! If you keep kicking or heading a football into your neighbour's garden, he won't be impressed by the fact that he might be living next to a soccer superstar of the future.

But if you can find a wall in a safe area, you can practise on your own or with friends to improve your shooting and passing skills. Here's a very simple exercise to improve the accuracy of your shooting.

Mark out a goal on the wall or fence, and divide it into eight equal rectangles (see fig. 6, overleaf). Number them, if you like. Select a particular zone of the goal, and try to kick the ball into it. If you hit the target, bring the ball under control as quickly as you can, and aim for another square. As your accuracy improves, try shooting from longer distances. But make sure that you are hitting a particular square regularly before you pass on to the next one.

69

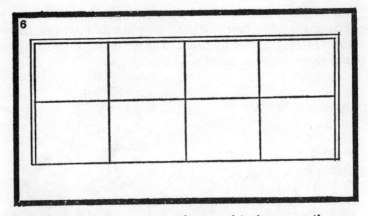

The lower squares can be used to improve the accuracy of your passing, particularly the side-footed **push pass**. Aim to keep the ball as low as possible, so that it raps against the angle formed by the ground and the wall.

Using the numbered squares, you can devise a useful game with a friend. Toss a coin. The player who wins the toss starts at square 1. If he hits it first time, he moves on to square 2. But if he misses, his opponent takes over, and so on. The first player to reach square 8, and find the target, wins the game. It won't take you long to think up variations on this basic game, but make sure that your practices involve aiming at a particular square, so that it is accuracy which counts in the end.

### The volley and the chip

The squared-off goal can also be used to practise some of the more difficult shots in football, particularly the **volley**. Using the volleying techniques described in Chapter 2, get a friend to toss the ball towards you at just above knee-height, as you stand with your right or left shoulder pointing towards the wall. See if you can volley the ball into a particular square. Vary the practice by facing the wall to start with, so that you have to turn and position yourself for the volley in a split-second, as you might be required to do in a match.

You could even have a shot at the **overhead volley** (fig. 7). But make sure that you've got something soft to land on, because you will land on your back if you execute the kick correctly! And that will be quite an achievement. Even professional players have difficulty in mastering the overhead volley. The trick is to allow the top half of your body to fall backwards, as you throw your legs into the air. As your foot finds contact with the ball, your hands and arms should be shaping to cushion the impact, as you hit the ground. But don't try this shot in a match until you have really

mastered it. If you are close to other players, a reckless, uncontrolled overhead volley may be regarded as dangerous play by the referee, and punished accordingly.

An equally devastating shot, and one which you should master as soon as possible, is the **chip**. The chip shot can be compared to a golf shot, in that your kicking foot should strike through the underside of the ball, in order to achieve lift and backspin. Professionals use the chip to float the ball over opponents, in situations where a ground pass would be easily intercepted. It can also be used with deadly effect against a goalkeeper who is coming off his line to narrow the angle.

The kick itself is more of a jabbing motion. You should be leaning backwards slightly, with the non-kicking foot slightly withdrawn from the ball, rather than alongside it (fig. 8). Keep your head down as your toe strikes through the bottom of the ball (fig. 9), and straighten your knee very quickly. Follow through with a full swing of the hip, with the leg fully extended.

You can use a wall to practise the chip shot, but the help of a couple of friends will be even more valuable. Two of you can practise chipping the ball to one another, while the third player stands in the middle, trying to cut off the lofted passes (fig. 10). But don't stand too far apart. The point of the chip shot is to gain height with the ball over short distances. Ideally, you should be able to 'chip' an opponent when you are only a few metres away from him.

## Group practices

Even the most dedicated young player needs the challenge of competition – the opportunity to compare his developing skills with a friend or relative. So try to persuade your Dad, or a few friends, to join in your practice sessions. Only three players are needed to carry out a wide range of exercises, passing movements, simple tactics and ball-games, for example the 'wall' pass (see Chapter 5) and speed off the mark.

To sharpen up your **speed** over short distances, one player moves slowly along a straight line with the

ball, while the other two keep pace on either side of him (fig. 11 on page 73). With a sudden, unexpected movement, the player in the middle passes the ball forward and sideways, for one of the flank players to chase. Perhaps the object is to stop the ball before it crosses a certain line. Or perhaps the ball is passed straight forward, so that the two outside players have to compete for it. The player in the middle could vary the practice by turning unexpectedly, forcing the others to check, and sprint back.

Another way to improve your speed off the mark (and inject a little fun into your training) is for all the available players to form a circle, spaced four or five metres apart. Start moving around the circle at a slow jog, until one of you lets out a sudden yell – the signal for every player to burst into a sprint. The object is to try and catch the player in front of you, by touching him with an outstretched arm. This is a particularly good practice for defenders who, in a match, may find themselves chasing a forward who has broken through. You could even turn the exercise into a lively game, by gradually eliminating the players who are caught and touched.

A circle can be used as the base for a wide range of routines and ball-games, which will help to relieve the boredom of training. For example, one player becomes 'piggy-in-the-middle', while the other two pass the ball to each other, back and forth across the circle (fig. 12). The chap in the middle tries to intercept the ball, forcing the players on the outside to employ a mixture of feints, sprints and dribbles, to work the ball past him. If you attempt to pass, and 'piggy' intercepts the ball, it's your turn to go in the middle.

When you get tired of this, stand some skittles or bottles in the middle of the circle. Then, using only one ball, spread out around the circle, and start shooting at the obstacles. Keep alert and on the move,

ready to cut off a shot from the player on the other side of the circle. Penalise the player who allows the ball to escape from the circle, and award yourself a point for knocking down a skittle. When all the skittles are down, the player with the highest number of points wins the Gold Medal!

The piggy-in-the-middle routine can also be used to improve your heading skills (fig. 13). The player in

the middle lobs the ball to the players on the outside, and then attempts to catch the ball as they head it to each other. Stand well apart, so that you have to get some power into your heading.

And what about a game of **head tennis**? Use a goal in the local park, if you can; or make your own 'tennis' net with a couple of poles and a length of string (fig. 14). Tie the string between the poles at a height of about two metres, and mark out a rough court, about 10 metres by 5 metres overall, if only two of you are taking part. Make the court proportionately larger if there are two or three players to each side. There's no need to stick to any rigid set of rules (unless you are playing in an official competition) as long as the ball is headed back and forth across the net, and is only allowed to bounce once after crossing the net.

Players can use their feet, thighs, head or chest to keep the ball in the air, passing it from man to man if necessary before heading it back across the net. If the ball is allowed to bounce twice, or is headed out of court, a point is awarded to the opposing team.

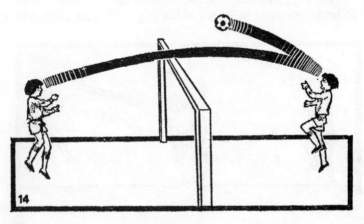

14

An inventive mind will soon devise more complicated rules. And no doubt many of you have already played head-tennis at school, or during training sessions with your local football club – games involving six players a side or even more. With enough players available, an expert soccer coach can devise an almost limitless range of complex training routines. But there is no room to discuss them here. The various practices we have discussed are designed to help a young player to make the best of his spare time, when there are no coaches or schoolteachers around to help him.

There are occasions when you have to get on and learn by yourself. And it's surprising how much you can learn with the aid of a wall, a football ... and a little help from your friends!

## Physical fitness

Working out a programme of physical training, and slogging through it on your own, requires a colossal effort of self-discipline. *But if you are not physically fit, all those hours of solitary practice may be utterly wasted.* All the skill in the world will count for little if you run out of stamina twenty minutes after the kick-off. You will just become a burden to your team-mates.

On the other hand, the player who goes into a match knowing that he can last the pace, will have a tremendous advantage over opponents of equal ability. He will be physically and mentally prepared for the game, brimming with confidence. Even professionals reach a point where they feel they cannot run another step, especially if the ground is heavy and the match has been fast and furious. But most of them are fit enough to recover quickly and get back into the game. Their skill is combined with stamina ... and the best way to improve your stamina is through regular stints of running training.

This doesn't mean that you've got to go charging off across the countryside until you fall flat on your face with exhaustion. During the ninety minutes of a football match, players sprint, jog, and even walk. Your running training should be broken up in the same way.

All you need is a football pitch in your local park. Imagine that the touchline is your running track. Start off at a steady jog, and run until you feel tired. Slow down to a walk. Once you get your breath back, start jogging again, then lunge into a sudden sprint. And so on. Use half the pitch, if you like. Mark out a triangle, and vary the exercise as before (fig. 15). Use the shortest side of the triangle for the sprints.

If you have never done any running training before, take it very easily at first. Stop immediately if you feel sick or distressed. Ease yourself into fitness and, hopefully, as the days and weeks pass, you will feel your stamina building up. You will be able to jog for longer and longer periods without getting tired. But it is vital that you continue to mix sprints with the longer runs, so that you achieve the ideal balance of fitness – the ability to produce those ten– and fifteen–

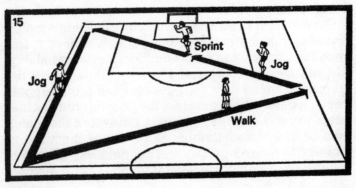

metre bursts throughout the ninety minutes of a football match.

Apart from running training, there are various simple exercises that you can perform at home. In addition to the exercises described in the chapter on Goalkeeping, you could try a few **sit-ups ...** or some **upside-down cycling** (see next two pages). If the weather is bad, and you can't get out into the park, a little running on the spot will help you to keep loosened up. Run slowly at first, gradually speeding up. And lift your knees as high as you can. Open the windows and breathe deeply, and if you can't use your bedroom, ask your parents for permission to train in the garage.

Take pride in your physical condition. The very fact that you are exercising, on your own, means that you are learning to discipline your mind as well as your body. You are teaching yourself to become the kind of player that any soccer coach would be glad to have in his squad.

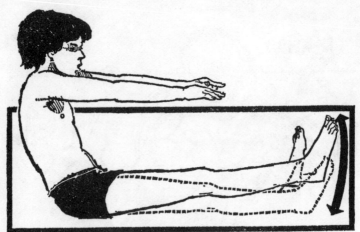

# 7  A CAREER IN FOOTBALL

If you dream of becoming a professional footballer, and you have the necessary talent, your dream could start coming true while you are still at school.

Let's imagine that you have just produced yet another stylish, eye-catching performance in a school match. At the end of the game, your games master introduces you to a complete stranger – a man who tells you that he is a scout for a professional football club. He likes the way you play, and wants to know if you would be interested in taking up football as a career. By the time the world stops spinning, you realise that the miracle has happened. You have been 'spotted'!

Of course, it doesn't always happen like this. You might attract the experienced eye of a scout while playing for a youth club, or for teams representing your town, or county, at various age-levels. Recognising your promise, the team manager (usually a

schoolmaster) will have recommended you to a club or a scout. From then on, you will be closely watched.

If the scout is impressed with your ability, he should first approach your youth club leader or school teacher, and then your parents. At this point it is vital – for your own protection – that your parents make a thorough check on the scout's credentials, and his links with the club that he claims to represent. If all seems well, you will then be invited to sign for the club on 'schoolboy forms'.

This means that you may not be approached by any other club without the permission of the club which has captured your signature. No more than that. You are still a long way from becoming a full-time professional.

During this 'probationary' period, the club will keep a close watch on your progress. You might take part in get-togethers or training sessions that the club arranges in your area, or be invited to the club's head-quarters to have a look round and get the 'feel' of a professional outfit.

If, at the age of sixteen, the club wishes to retain its interest in you, you will be invited to join the club as an apprentice professional.

Again, your parents should explore the situation thoroughly, so that they are aware of all the implications. Remember that a football apprenticeship is completely different from a trade apprenticeship. In the end, your skills and dedication are the only factors which will bring success.

But you have got this far, and nothing can dissuade you, so you sign the registration form. To begin with, you will be paid a nominal weekly wage of about £12, plus accommodation expenses if you have to move away from your home town. But try not to worry too much about money at this stage. The pride and excitement of belonging to a professional football club should more than make up for the modest financial rewards. Even the highly-paid Johan Cruyff had to start at the bottom.

## And so to work

A day in the life of an apprentice begins around 9.15, when he arrives at the stadium for the morning 'stint'. And he will probably be put straight to work.

If told to assist the groundsman, he may find himself helping to remove divots from the pitch, clearing litter from the terraces, or even swabbing down the showers. He is also expected to clean out the dressing-rooms after each training session, and look after the personal gear of the senior professionals. In some clubs, each apprentice is responsible for maintaining the kit of, say, three of the senior players. He must ensure that their boots, training-shoes and spikes are thoroughly cleaned, and their strip sent to the laundry.

Such tasks will seem tedious and frustrating to the eager young player who has only one ambition in life – to play football. But they must be carried out cheerfully, and to the best of his ability. There is no place for a lazy apprentice in the hectic world of a busy football club. And there will be plenty of football, never fear!

Apart from training, coaching sessions and full-scale practice matches, apprentices usually take part in league and cup games about twice a week. These days few clubs outside the First Division can afford to run teams consisting wholly of apprentices, so you may find yourself playing alongside more experienced professionals in the club's 'A' side, or even the reserves. Obviously, the club manager will want to see you making as much progress as possible, and will not hesitate to draft an apprentice into the first team if he thinks the young player is good enough.

But even as he strives for success as a footballer, the wise apprentice will be thinking about the future. Always bear in mind that you can't keep on playing football until you are sixty-five.

An injury could bring your playing career to a premature end, and some of our greatest players have retired whilst still at their peak, restricting themselves to exhibition games, and benefit matches. So it is vital to prepare yourself for an alternative career, outside the game.

The club will help by allowing apprentices to attend the nearest technical college – perhaps twice a week – where they may study a wide range of subjects and careers.

The opportunity is there, and it would be foolish to waste it. For a rising young player, the knowledge that

he can earn a good living when his playing days are over must be a source of confidence which will colour his game, and make him a better footballer.

## The moment of truth

This usually occurs for an apprentice on or around his eighteenth birthday, for then the club must either sign him on as a full professional or release his registration. In other words, he is out of a job. He must try his luck with another club, or forget about a career in football.

For those apprentices who have made the grade, and are offered a full- or part-time contract, the sky is the limit. Nowadays, the top players can negotiate contracts for themselves worth many thousands of pounds per year. Some of them even have their own agents and fan-clubs, and swell their income through various 'perks', such as advertising.

But if life seems to have dealt you a cruel blow, and thrown you on to the soccer scrap-heap, don't despair! Even if you are not offered an apprenticeship or, later, a contract, there is a good chance that you may find your way back into the professional game through various other levels of football, such as amateur or non-league clubs. And think of the virtually unknown players who have gone to North America, and other parts of the world where football is booming, and succeeded in establishing themselves as stars.

So if you think that you have the ability to succeed, keep trying! Believe in yourself, be willing to learn, and devote every spare moment to mastering the skills of football. And you may yet achieve the satisfaction of earning a living from your favourite sport.

# 8 THE MAN IN CHARGE

We can't all be good footballers, or even moderately good footballers. Some of us will never make any real impact on the game as a player, no matter how hard we practise. But it's nothing to be ashamed of. It takes all sorts to make a football match, and the man who has to control the game can contribute as much to a clean, exciting, fast-flowing game of soccer as the twenty-two players. So why not think seriously about becoming a referee?

Efficient referees are in constant demand at all levels of football, and there is no better way of remaining actively involved in your favourite sport. All you need, to begin with, is a copy of the Laws of Association Football. Learn the rules of the game from back to front, and inside out. Then contact the secretary of your local Referees' Society, and tell him that you are interested in becoming a referee. Don't be put off because of your age. Even if you are only twelve years old, you will probably be welcomed with open arms, and invited to attend a course on refereeing. The course usually lasts for about eight weeks, and is followed by a written exam. If you can pass it, you are on the way to becoming a Class 3 Referee.

You cannot register with your County Association as a Class 3 referee until you are sixteen. In the meantime, you can gain valuable experience by acting as linesman in local 'parks' football, or officiating at junior school matches. The thrill of refereeing your first school match will never be forgotten.

From the age of sixteen – when you will be allowed to referee senior local amateur games – your progress will depend on how well you impress the assessors. This means that your performance with the whistle will be 'assessed' and marked by panels of experts over, say, half-a-dozen matches. If you reach the required standard, you will be 'promoted' to a higher grade of football, and allowed to run the line in senior amateur league competitions, such as the London Spartan League. Again, you will be watched and assessed, until you are considered proficient enough to 'take' a game as referee.

This process of assessment and promotion is continued all the way up through the various grades of football until, with hope and perseverance, you may find yourself officiating as linesman at a top, professional football match. Even at this stage in an official's career, there is still a lot of work to be done before he becomes a full Football League referee, but the effort and dedication is worthwhile. The men who referee European and World Cup games are chosen by F.I.F.A. from officials who are recommended by the member nations. So the 'man in the middle', if he is good enough, has an opportunity to tread the most famous football pitches in the world.

To be a good referee, you must be physically fit – fit enough to withstand the pace of a modern, ninety-minute game, in any kind of weather.

You must have the courage to make your decisions firmly and correctly, in a manner that will command the respect of both players and spectators. You must, of course, be absolutely fair and impartial in everything you do. And above all, you must have a *thorough knowledge and understanding of the laws of football*.

Test your knowledge of the game with the following questions. They say that the odds against a referee becoming a World Cup Finals official are about 30,000–1. But if you can answer more than half the questions without taking a sneaky glance or two at the Laws . . . well, you never know.

You will find the answers on page 92.

## Questions

1 What should be the maximum and minimum weight of a football at start of play?

2 A football match starts when the referee blows his whistle for the kick-off. True or false?

3 Can a player be sent off before a game starts?

4 Is a captain obliged to take choice of ends on winning the toss?

5 Linesmen can give decisions. True or false?

6 If a player is in an off-side position, and he receives the ball direct from a goal-kick, what is the referee's decision?

7 What are the nine offences which are punishable by a penalty-kick, if intentionally committed by a player in his own penalty-area?

8 What is the referee's decision if the ball strikes the *half-way flag*, and rebounds into play?

9 Dangerous play is penalised by a direct free-kick. True or false?

10 How close can you stand to an opponent who is taking a throw-in?

**11** If, when taking a throw-in, you throw the ball *directly* into your *opponents*' goal, what is the correct decision?

**12** What is the correct decision if you throw the ball directly into your *own* goal?

**13** If a player, when taking a free-kick, plays the ball a second time before it has touched another player, can he be penalised?

**14** Imagine that you have drawn the goalkeeper, and slipped the ball past him. But a spectator rushes on to the pitch and kicks the ball away before it can enter the net. What is the referee's decision?

**15** You are taking a free-kick from outside your own penalty-area, and you decide to pass the ball back to your goalkeeper. To your horror, the ball misses him and rolls into the net. Is it a goal to the opposing side?

**16** If you are unlucky enough to have Pushy Pete as a team-mate, and he uses your shoulders as a springboard when jumping to head the ball, how would the referee deal with him?

**17** A goal-bound shot hits the referee, causing the ball to deflect past the goalkeeper and into the net. What is the correct decision?

**18** A winger takes a corner, and the ball strikes the near upright before rebounding back to him. He crosses the ball again, and one of his team-mates heads the ball into the net. Is it a goal?

**19** Can a referee, after blowing for half-time, demand that the teams change over, and restart the game immediately?

**20** The ball beats the goalkeeper, but bursts or becomes deflated before it enters the net. What is the referee's decision?

**21** Finally, here is a word of warning. Can a player be sent off the field, even though he may not have been 'shown the yellow card' for a previous offence?

## Answers

1 Although a football may lose pressure during a game, it should weigh not less than 14 oz and not more than 16 oz at start of play.

2 False. The referee merely gives the *signal* for the game to begin. The ball is not in play until it has travelled the distance of its own circumference, in a *forward* direction.

3 Yes. A player can be dismissed from the field of play before the kick-off, if, in the opinion of the referee, he is guilty of violent conduct, or uses foul or abusive language.

4 No. He can choose to kick off instead.

5 False. Linesmen may only *indicate* to the referee that the ball has gone out of play, or that a breach in the Laws of the game has occurred. It is the referee's job to award throws-in, goal-kicks, corner-kicks, and free-kicks.

6 Play on! A player cannot be off-side if he receives the ball direct from a goal-kick, a corner-kick, a throw-in, or when the ball is dropped by the referee.

7 (a) kicking, or attempting to kick an opponent;

(b) tripping an opponent;

(c) jumping at an opponent;

(d) charging an opponent in a violent or dangerous manner;

(e) striking or attempting to strike an opponent;

(f) holding an opponent;

(g) charging an opponent from behind, unless the latter be obstructing;

(h) pushing an opponent;

(i) handling the ball (this does not, of course, apply to the goalkeeper within his own penalty-area).

8 A throw-in! The flag-sticks that mark the half-way line are positioned *outside* the field of play – at least, they *should* be!

9 False. Dangerous play is penalised by an *indirect* free-kick, even though the offence may be committed by a defender within his own penalty-area.

10 Technically, you can stand as close as you like, as long as you do not move, or gesticulate in a manner that is calculated to distract or impede the thrower.

11 A goal-kick.

12 A corner-kick to the opposing side.

13 Yes. The penalty is an indirect free-kick, to the opposing team, to be taken from the spot where the infringement occurred.

14 The referee must stop the game, and restart it with a dropped ball at the spot where the incident occurred.

15 No! To your great relief, the referee's decision is a corner to your opponents.

16 The referee should stop the game, caution Pete for ungentlemanly conduct, and award an indirect free-kick to your opponents.

17 A goal, because the referee is regarded as part of the field of play.

18 No. The referee must award a free-kick against the winger, because he has played the ball twice before another player has touched it.

19 He can *request*, but not demand. Players are entitled to a five-minute break at half-time, under the Laws of the game.

20 No goal. The referee restarts the game by dropping the new ball at the place where the first ball became defective.

21 Yes. If, in the opinion of the referee, a player is guilty of violent conduct, serious foul play, or abusive language, he may be dismissed from the game without first receiving a caution.

# 9 TAKING CARE OF WHAT YOU WEAR

Choosing and buying football equipment can be a costly and bewildering business. Almost every sports shop carries a vast range of boots, footballs, strips and track-suits. Adidas, Admiral, Patrick and Puma are just a few of the manufacturers competing for your precious cash.

In general, the cost of your equipment will be determined by its quality. Football boots, for example, can cost as little as £4.50 or as much as £30. So it's best to 'shop around', as they say. And it will help you to spend your money wisely, if you know something about the various items of equipment that you are planning to buy.

## Boots

It may surprise you to know that the Laws of the game do not insist that boots, or shoes, *must* be worn. A player can wear what he likes on his feet, as long as his footwear doesn't upset his manager, and complies with the requirements of Law 4.

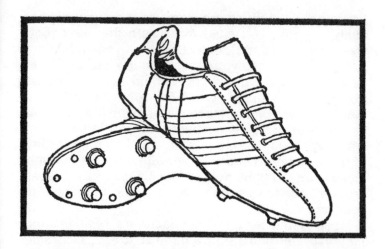

But let's assume that you are already using the familiar, studded boot; and if you want a pair that will withstand the rigours of our all-weather season, then there is no substitute for leather. Boots with vinyl uppers, ranging from £4.50 to £6.50 according to size, are also available. But it should be remembered that vinyl tends to split and crack more easily, particularly when subjected to extremes of temperature. So if you can afford it, buy boots with leather uppers.

Whether you choose a boot with a *moulded* sole or a *screw-in* sole, is entirely up to you. Both types are available in cheap and expensive styles. But if you can afford a boot which takes screw-in studs, you have the advantage of being able to change your studs to suit the playing conditions. The Law states that replacement studs should be made of rubber, aluminium, leather, plastic or similar materials. They must be solid, and should not project more than ¼ inch from the sole.

Whichever type of boot you prefer (and remember that you might as well throw away a pair of moulded boots once the studs are worn, because you cannot change them), you must make sure that your footwear is supple and flexible. Boots with soles that are too rigid can impair your 'touch' on the ball, and even cause injury. So the fitting should be as snug as possible, particularly across the width of your foot. And if you are one of those players who likes to wear two pairs of socks, remember to take this into account when trying on a new pair of boots. Aim for a feeling of overall comfort and support, with the insteps firmly laced – not too tight, not too loose. Don't tie the laces around your ankles, because this will interfere with your mobility.

Most of the leading manufacturers offer leather, moulded-sole boots from around £6 to £22, according to size and styling. Boots of reasonable quality with screw-in soles can be obtained for as little as £8.50.

Like all the prices that you see quoted in this chapter, these are approximate figures, which may vary slightly from one shop to another. And don't forget to allow for our old enemy, inflation! The cost of sports equipment is rising all the time, so it's vital that you get as much wear out of your boots as possible. The folly of allowing a pair of perfectly good boots to wear out in a matter of months, because you have failed to look after them properly, must be obvious to everyone. Except, perhaps ... players like Pushy Pete.

### Maintenance of boots

If you are as sloppy and uncaring as Pushy Pete, you will probably drag off your muddy boots at the end of a match, throw them into a bag along with the rest of your gear, and forget about them until the next match or training session. Even good-quality leather will suffer from such treatment.

At the end of each game, you should first remove

as much mud and dirt from your boots as you can, then put them in a plastic bag or wrap them in newspaper. This will ensure that your boots do not soil the rest of your gear. At home, clean your boots more thoroughly with a soft brush and a damp cloth, then hang them up to dry. Allow the boots to dry slowly, at normal room temperature. Do not put them in the airing cupboard, or stand them in front of the fire.

After a day or two, give the boots a good coating of dubbin, wax polish or boot polish. This will keep the leather pliable, and provide all-weather protection. Never use oil or detergents on your boots. From time to time, check your studs. Badly-worn studs can cause injury to other players, and broken studs of the screw-in type should be replaced immediately. Finally, when your boots are not in use, stuff them with newspaper to help them to hold their shape.

Follow these simple rules regularly and carefully, and you will get the best out of your football boots. At least, they are unlikely to fall apart in the middle of a game . . . like Pushy Pete's!

# Strip

Even if you play regularly for a team that provides shirts and shorts, many of you may prefer to buy your own strip; perhaps in the colours of your favourite professional club. But don't just buy any pair of shorts or socks that take your fancy. Make sure that they fit you properly, because ill-fitting gear can interfere with your blood circulation.

## Shirts

Look for shirts made in hard-wearing, 'honeycomb' materials: cotton or polyester. These fabrics wash well, and mould comfortably to your body-shape. Prices range from £2.50 upwards, according to size.

## Shorts

Make sure that your shorts are not too tight, and have a wide waist-band containing three bands of elastic. Cotton shorts tend to lose their colour, and shrink when washed, so it's best to choose washable nylon. Prices range from £1.75 to £5.

## Socks

Nylon is the material to go for. It keeps its shape, doesn't shrink, and the colours are fast. Woollen socks soon become baggy, and are not really worth the expense. Expect to pay from £1.25 upwards for a good pair of socks.

## Pads

Unless pads make you feel really uncomfortable and restrict your game, it is sensible to wear them. Pads made of cane and horsehair are still available, but they are not shaped to your leg, and tend to move around under your stocking. You can buy the cheapest pads of this type for around 70p.

Nylon, foam-backed pads are more expensive, ranging from £1.25 to £3.75. On the other hand, these are shaped, and will give you greater comfort and mobility.

## Track-suits

Don't confuse track-suits with training suits or leisure suits. For training purposes, the track-suit with narrow leggings and stirrup-type fitting is still quite adequate. Leggings with flared bottoms may look fashionable, but they can pick up a lot of mud.

Younger players can buy 'small-size' suits, of average quality, for about £5.50. For the older player, there is a wide range of track-suits starting at around £8.50 and rising to £12.

## Goalkeepers' jerseys

There is little to choose between the various makes which are available. There are 'economy range' jerseys and expensive jerseys. Some firms will even make a jersey to your own design, provided you choose from a specific range of colours. It all depends on what you can afford.

## Training shoes

It has become fashionable to wear training shoes for various leisure activities, apart from football; so you will need a strong pair, preferably made of leather. Prices range from £5 to £15, according to size and quality.

## Footballs

You can pay up to £30 for a top quality football, made of coated leather and hand-sewn. On the other hand, footballs imported from some Far East countries can cost as little as £3, but don't be surprised if they lose their shape after a season's wear! A ball of good, average quality, made of synthetic leather, will cost you about £8, and it will hold its shape well ... as long as you look after it! Even leather balls which have a water-repellent coating should be thoroughly washed after use. Uncoated balls need a regular application of dubbin.

And so we come back to *care and maintenance*. Try not to think of it as a boring chore. If you take the time and trouble to keep your kit looking clean and smart, you will prolong its life and be better off financially.

And if you look good, you will almost certainly feel good – ready to run rings round all those scruffy Pushy Petes, who haven't bothered to look after their gear.

# 10  HOW IT ALL BEGAN

You open your daily newspaper one morning, and an amazing headline leaps at you from the sports section:

### THE GOVERNMENT BLOWS THE WHISTLE ON AFTER-SCHOOL SOCCER

*By our Educational Correspondent*

Alarmed by the way more and more children are putting football before homework, and neglecting their 'O' and 'A' level studies, the Government has slapped a nation-wide ban on our national game. As from today, boys – and girls – within the 11–16 age group found playing football outside school hours, will be liable to heavy fines (deductible from their pocket money) and their football equipment confiscated....

What a horrifying prospect! But before you start saying that it could never happen, consider the plight of football fanatics during Edward II's reign. In fear that great 'evils' might sweep the country, the King placed a royal ban on football, because the peasants were neglecting their archery practice!

So you see, football was having a big impact on everyday life even as long ago as the fourteenth century. The first records of football being played in England date back to 1175, but a form of football called Tsu Chu (kick-ball) was played in China over two thousand years ago. The Greeks called it 'episkyros', and still another version of the game, known as 'harpastum', was brought to Britain by the Romans.

Despite attempts by various monarchs to outlaw it, football continued to flourish in England during the fifteenth and sixteenth centuries. But it was limited to

'mob' games, with up to five hundred players on each side: one village, or town, against another!

Scores of people were injured, and even killed, in the course of a single game. It's no wonder contemporary writers condemned football as a murderous, blood-letting brawl.

It was not until the early part of the nineteenth century, when football became popular at our public schools and universities, that the game became more organised, and attempts were made to find a common set of rules. By October 1863, when the Football Association was formed, the ball could still be handled, as well as kicked, but it was a dispute over the rule relating to 'hacking' that led to the withdrawal of some of the founder clubs, and the formation of the Rugby Union, in 1871.

From then on, 'soccer' – as football was called, to distinguish it from rugger – began to develop into the exciting, tactical game that we know today. On 16th March, 1872, a crowd of about two thousand people saw Wanderers beat the Royal Engineers, 1–0, in the first F.A. Cup final at Kennington Oval. The success of the competition led to more and more county and district associations being formed, even though some players still wore caps and knicker-bockers, and the referee sometimes dressed in his everyday clothes and carried a walking stick!

By 1882, the number of clubs entering for the F.A. Cup competition had increased to 73, and over 110,000 fans swarmed into the Crystal Palace ground to watch the 1901 final between Tottenham Hotspur and Sheffield United.

The increasing number of professional players in the game led to the formation of the Football League in 1888. In the first season, only twelve teams took part, and it was not until 1894 that the Southern League was formed. Many clubs in the south were

bitterly opposed to the idea of players being actually paid to kick a football.

But nothing could halt the march of our 'simplest' game. The Scottish League had been formed in 1889, and the Irish in 1890, and the powerful Southern League became the Third Division of the Football League in 1921.

Although it is the F.A. Cup competition which generates the glamour and excitement foreseen by those dedicated organisers and officials of the nineteenth century, the real strength of football lies in the weekly nation-wide programme of League football – a vast, intricately-organised sporting spectacle, which has its roots in that obscure game of Tsu Chu which the Chinese played over two thousand years ago.

# Football goes international

Only about two thousand people watched the first official International Football Match between England and Scotland in 1872. The game took place at Hamilton Crescent, Partick ... on a cricket field! Today, crowds of up to 100,000 welcome teams such as Italy and Brazil to Wembley Stadium, thanks largely to the soldiers, sailors and businessmen who helped to spread the magic of football across the world during the latter part of the nineteenth century. They took their footballs to Europe, South America, Brazil and even Russia, where the Tsarist authorities feared that football clubs might be used as a breeding-ground for revolution!

More and more countries formed their own national associations, and in 1904, F.I.F.A. (the Federation Internationale de Football Association) was formed. More than 140 national associations are now affiliated to F.I.F.A., including the United Kingdom associations, which joined in 1946. In October 1902, Austria played Hungary in the first international match between non-British countries, but at home the main interest still centred on the stirring annual battles between the old enemies, England and Scotland.

England hold the edge in matches played at Hampden Park, but Scotland's most famous victory was achieved at Wembley, with a team that will be forever known as the 'Wembley Wizards'. The tiny Scottish attackers tore England apart with a smooth, silky blend of close-passing and dribbling, and stormed to a sensational 5–1 victory.

As far as foreign teams were concerned, however, England reigned supreme at Wembley. No European nation had ever defeated us on our own soil. Not until November 25th, 1953, that is, when the 'Magic Magyars' of Hungary arrived with an irresistible style of football that stunned the world of soccer. England 3, Hungary 6 was the incredible result! Football would never be the same again. The Hungarians had crushed the complacency of our invincible years, and taught our managers and coaches that there was more to preparing for a football match than a few press-ups and a couple of sprints around the running track.

## The World Cup

Thanks to television, the European Champions Cup, the European Cup-Winners Cup and the U.E.F.A. Cup are all familiar and exciting milestones in the European soccer season. At international level, there is also the European Football Championship, which was formerly known as the Nations Cup. But in terms of glamour, sheer excitement and world-wide interest, none of these competitions can compare with the World Cup soccer tournament.

The British countries declined to take part in the pre-War tournaments, and there were only thirteen entries for the first tournament in 1930, when the Jules Rimet trophy was won by Uruguay. Italy won the next two tournaments, in 1934 and 1938, and twelve years elapsed before the next World Cup competition was held in Brazil, with England taking part for the first time. And what a humiliating disaster it turned out to be! In one of the most incredible soccer upsets of all time, England were beaten 1–0 by the United States.

England paraded a galaxy of stars, but went down to an American team captained by Eddie McIlvenny, who had been given a free transfer by Third Division Wrexham! The trophy was eventually won by Uruguay, after a momentous match against Brazil in front of 200,000 spectators.

In 1954, Hungary were expected to walk away with

the trophy. Three weeks before the tournament, the 'Magyars' had thrashed England, 7-1. But the team which had not lost a game in four years were beaten 3-2 by West Germany in a sensational final.

In the 1958 tournament, England put up another dismal performance, although Wales reached the quarter-finals. It took a rather fortunate goal, scored by a certain player called Pele, to put them out. Brazil went on to win the trophy in 1958 and again in 1962, playing brilliant 'samba soccer' that no other country could match.

And so to 1966! And that never-to-be-forgotten day in July, when England and West Germany marched out to contest the final of the World Cup at Wembley Stadium. The England team was as follows:

Banks

Cohen    J. Charlton    Moore    Wilson

Stiles    R. Charlton    Peters

Ball    Hunt    Hurst

The England manager, Sir Alf Ramsey, had decided to play without orthodox wingers, and dispensed with individualist goal-poachers like Jimmy Greaves. He seemed to be hoping that colossal 'work-rate' would compensate for a lack of outstanding players in his squad. But England had three players approaching world-class in Bobby Charlton, Bobby Moore and Gordon Banks. So perhaps it is not so surprising that they battled through to the final after an uneasy start, and put England back on top of the football world, with a 4–2 victory over West Germany after extra time. Hardened soccer fans literally cried with joy as Bobby Moore and his men took the Jules Rimet trophy on lap after lap of honour.

Geoff Hurst became the first player to score a hat-trick in a World Cup final, and players like Alan

Ball, Nobby Stiles and Martin Peters emerged as heroes.

Many experts believe that only the absence of Gordon Banks prevented England reaching the semifinals of the 1970 World Cup, which was held in Mexico. Brazil defeated Italy 4–1 in the final, and claimed the Jules Rimet trophy outright.

Since then, the FIFA World Cup is now the premier prize in soccer. West Germany won it in 1974, and we all know how narrowly, and tragically England failed to reach the final stages of the 1978 tournament, which was, of course, won by Argentina.

But the recent performances of all the home countries hold out hope for the future. Managers and coaches throughout Britain seem to be coming round to the realisation that speed and work-rate must be balanced with that vital ingredient called skill. If all these qualities can be blended into a style of football that is uniquely British, then ... who knows? Perhaps, in the next World Cup tournament, one of the United Kingdom teams – the English, the Scots, the Welsh or the Irish – will fashion a repeat of that great day, in 1966, when Wembley Stadium became the shrine of football.

# 11  A MINE OF INFORMATION

Has any other player, apart from Pele, scored more than 1000 goals during his soccer career? How many times have Real Madrid won the European Cup? Who scored six goals in an F.A. Cup match, and still finished on the losing side?

You will find the answers to these questions somewhere in this chapter, along with a selection of facts and figures drawn from the fascinating statistics of soccer. A full account of the amazing, intriguing, record-breaking feats of football would provide enough material to fill a miniature encyclopedia, but you should find enough information within the next few pages to settle some of those endless arguments with friends and parents.

## Nicknames

The names or nicknames of many European and South American clubs have become world famous – the 'Grasshoppers' of Zurich, for example. Or the 'Eagles' of Benfica. The Russian 'Dynamos' of Moscow and Kiev appear regularly in European competitions. In Argentina, the supporters of the River Plate club pay homage to 'The Machine'. And what about the 'Billygoats' for an unusual nickname? It belongs to the West German club, F.C. Köln. West Germany also has its 'Red Devils', in the shape of Kaiserslautern.

But no doubt you will be able to track down many more weird and wonderful nicknames. Just to whet your appetitie, which Scottish club is affectionately called 'The Loons' by its fans? Who are the 'Accies'? Where are the 'Minster Men' to be found?

Once you get started, you might even become a soccer statistic yourself, by collecting the nicknames of every professional football club in the world!

Let's take the first step along the road to becoming a Soccer Superbrain by having a look at the nicknames of some of the better-known British and European clubs.

| | |
|---|---|
| Aberdeen .. .. | 'Dons' |
| Arsenal .. .. .. | 'Gunners' |
| Aston Villa .. .. | 'Villains' |
| Birmingham C. .. | 'Blues' |
| Blackburn Rovers .. | 'Rovers' or 'Blue & Whites' |
| Bolton .. .. .. | 'Trotters' |
| Brighton .. .. .. | 'Seagulls' |
| Bristol City .. .. | 'Robins' |
| Bristol Rovers .. | 'Pirates' |
| Burnley .. .. .. | 'Clarets' |
| Cardiff City .. .. | 'Bluebirds' |
| Celtic .. .. .. | 'Bhoys' |
| Charlton .. .. .. | 'Haddicks', 'Robins' or 'Vallants' |
| Chelsea .. .. .. | 'Blues' |
| Coventry .. .. .. | 'Sky Blues' |
| Crystal Palace.. .. | 'Eagles' |
| Derby County .. .. | 'Rams' |
| Dundee United .. | 'Terrors' |
| Everton .. .. .. | 'Toffeemen' or 'Blues' |
| Fulham .. .. .. | 'Cottagers' |
| Heart of Midlothian.. | 'Hearts' |
| Hibernian .. .. .. | 'Hibs' |
| Ipswich .. .. .. | 'Town' |
| Leicester City .. .. | 'Filberts' or 'Foxes' or 'City' |
| Liverpool .. .. | 'Reds' or 'Pool' |
| Luton Town .. .. | 'Hatters' |
| Manchester City .. | 'Citizens' or 'City' |

| | |
|---|---|
| Manchester United | 'Red Devils' |
| Middlesbrough .. | 'Boro' |
| Millwall .. .. .. | 'Lions' |
| Morton .. .. .. | 'Ton' |
| Motherwell .. .. | 'Well' |
| Newcastle United .. | 'Magpies' |
| Norwich City .. | 'Canaries' |
| Nottingham Forest | 'Reds' |
| Notts County .. .. | 'Magpies' |
| Oldham .. .. .. | 'Latics' |
| Orient .. .. .. | 'O's' |
| Partick Thistle .. | 'Jags' |
| Preston North End | 'Lillywhites' or 'North End' |
| Queens Park Rangers | 'Rangers' or 'R's' |
| Rangers .. .. .. | 'Blues' or 'Gers' |
| Sheffield United .. | 'Blades' |
| Sheffield Wednesday | 'Owls' |
| Southampton .. | 'Saints' |
| St Mirren .. .. | 'Buddies' |
| Stoke City.. .. .. | 'Potters' |
| Sunderland .. .. | 'Rokerites' |
| Tottenham Hotspur | 'Spurs' |
| West Bromwich Albion .. | 'Throstles' or 'Albion' |
| West Ham United .. | 'Hammers' or 'Irons' |
| Wolverhampton Wanderers | 'Wolves' |
| Wrexham .. .. | 'Robins' |

## Goals galore

The business of scoring goals has produced a spectacular crop of facts and figures.

When Arbroath played Bon Accord in a Scottish Cup Match in September 1885, Arbroath won 36–0! This is still the highest score recorded in a British first-class match. The record for an International match is England 17, Australia 0. The game took place in Sydney in 1951; although it is not listed by England as a full International.

In 1887, Preston North End beat Hyde 26–0 at Deepdale, Lancs, to set up the record for an F.A. Cup match. The biggest victory ever recorded in an F.A. Cup final is 6–0, when Bury beat Derby County at Crystal Palace in 1903.

The record for a Scottish final is Renton 6, Cambuslang 1, in 1888. Celtic beat Hibernian by the same score in 1972.

West Bromwich Albion, Notts Forest and Aston Villa share the record for the highest number of goals scored by one side in a Football League (Division 1) match. Albion thrashed Darwen 12–0 in 1892, Forest beat Leicester Fosse by the same score in 1909, and Villa destroyed Accrington 12–2, in 1892.

Celtic trounced Dundee 11–0 in 1895 to establish a Scottish Division 1 record, and Hibernian equalled it by beating Airdrie 11–1 in 1959.

### Individual performances

A player called Stanis holds the record for the most goals scored by one player in a first class match. He found the net 16 times for Racing Club de Lens against Aubry-Asturies in December 1942. The greatest number of goals attributed to one player in an International match is 10, scored by Gottfried Fuchs, when Germany beat Russia 16–0 in the 1912 Olympic Tournament.

John Petrie holds the record for British first-class matches. He scored 13 times against Bon Accord.

Ted 'Drake hit 7 goals for Arsenal against Aston Villa in 1935, to set up an English First Division record. But Joe Payne holds the Football League record for any division. He scored an incredible 10 goals against Bristol Rovers for Luton Town in April 1936.

In January 1928, the legendary James McGrory hit 8 goals for Celtic against Dunfermline Athletic, to clinch the Scottish First Division record.

The individual goal-scoring record for a British home International match is held by Joe Bambrick, who scored 6 goals for Ireland against Wales at Belfast in February 1930.

And that player who scored 6 goals in an F.A. Cup match, and still finished up on the losing side? It was Dennis Law. He had scored all 6 of Manchester City's goals against Luton Town in a 4th round match, when the game was abandoned during a downpour, with City leading 6–2. Luton won the replay, 3–1. And guess who scored City's only goal? That's right ... Dennis Law!

## Career and season totals

Artur Friedenreich, who was born in 1892, is credited with scoring a fantastic 1329 goals in Brazilian football. But the record for the greatest number of *documented* goals is held by Edson Arantes do Nascimento, otherwise known as Pele. Between 1956 and 1974 he scored 1216 goals in 1254 games. Pele scored 139 goals in 1958, and his total had climbed to 1281 by the time he retired in October 1977.

The only other player to score more than 1000 goals in his career is Franz Binder. He notched up 1006 goals in the course of 756 games played in Austria and Germany, between 1930 and 1950.

The British career record is held by Glasgow Celtic's James McGrory. He scored 550 goals in first class matches, 410 of them in Scottish League games.

The most goals scored in English League matches is 434, by Arthur Rowley. He also scored 32 goals in F.A. Cup matches. Jimmy Greaves holds the English First Division record with 357 goals.

Such an avalanche of goals would not be complete without mentioning the great Dixie Dean, who scored a total of 82 goals in a single season. His record-breaking feat embraced League, Cup and representative matches, and included a Football League record of 60 goals in 39 games.

A prolific scorer in the post-war years was Ferenk Deak. He hit 66 goals for Szentlorinci AC in Hungary in 1945–46, 48 in 1946–47, and an astonishing 59 goals for Ferencvaros in 1948–49.

And let us not forget Arnold Birch of Chesterfield, who set up a Football League record in 1923–24. His total for the season? Just 5 goals! But then Arnold was a goalkeeper, and all his goals came from penalties!

## Football 'firsts'

You will find some of football's most important 'firsts' in the chapter entitled 'How it all began' ... but the history of soccer is scattered with intriguing milestones.

The first Football League games were played on September 8th, 1888. Cox, of Aston Villa, is recorded as scoring the first 'own goal'.

King George V became the first reigning monarch to watch a Cup Final, when he attended the Burnley v Liverpool game in 1914.

England suffered their first defeat on foreign soil when they lost 4–1 to Spain in Madrid in 1929.

The first Football League match to be played under floodlights took place at Fratton Park, Portsmouth, in February 1956, although two Sheffield Association teams played under a form of floodlighting, at Bramall Lane, as long ago as 1878.

The first hat-trick in an F.A. Cup final was scored by William Townley for Blackburn Rovers against Sheffield Wednesday in 1890.

Shinguards were first introduced by Sam Widdowson of Notts Forest in 1874.

An estimated 100,000 fans packed into Stamford Bridge in November 1945, to watch Chelsea play Moscow Dynamo, the first Russian team to visit Britain. The result was a 3–3 draw.

On August 21st, 1965, Keith Peacock of Charlton Athletic became the first player to appear in a Football League match as a substitute. On the same day, Barrow's Bobby Know became the first substitute to actually score a goal in a Football League game against Wrexham.

In their first season as a League club in 1960–61, Peterborough United scored 134 goals in 46 matches, which is still a record for the English League.

The first match to be played on a full-sized pitch completely under cover took place in the Houston Astrodome in Texas, in April 1967, between Real Madrid and West Ham United.

But perhaps the most satisfying football first was achieved by Newcastle United's Billy Foulkes. In his first International match for Wales against England, in October 1951, Foulkes scored with his first kick!

## Football 'mosts'

Aston Villa have won the F.A. Cup the most times – in 1887, 1895, 1897, 1905, 1913, 1920 and 1957. Newcastle have won the Cup six times, and appeared in the Final eleven times.

Villa have also registered the most League Cup wins – in 1961, 1975 and 1977.

The most League Championship (Division 1) wins is 10, by Liverpool, in 1901, 1906, 1922, 1923, 1947, 1964, 1966, 1973, 1976, and 1977.

Bobby Charlton holds the career-record for the most goals scored by an England International, with

49; although his total falls well short of the 90 goals scored by Pele for Brazil.

Some of Pele's goals have helped Brazil to win the World Cup the most times. Apart from appearing in the finals of every World Cup competition, Brazil won the tournament in 1958, 1962 and 1970.

Gerd Muller of West Germany, with 14, holds the record for most goals in World Cup Finals. The most goals scored in a Final is 3, by England's Geoff Hurst.

In the European Champions Cup, Real Madrid have won the trophy the most times, in 1956, '57, '58, '59 and '60, and again in 1966 – an incredible soccer 'most' which may never be bettered.

## Highest and lowest

The highest transfer fee ever paid for a single player is £1.5m. It was paid by Vicenta to Juventus for Paolo Rossi in May, 1978. A reported £1.4m was paid by Napoli to Bologna for Giuseppe Savoldi in 1975, but the deal included two other players.

The highest fee received by a British club is £975,000, paid by Nottingham Forest to Birmingham City for Trevor Francis, in February, 1979. V.A.T. and other items boosted the final figure to approximately £1,150,500.

Compare these colossal sums with the fee paid by Middlesborough to Sunderland in 1905, for Alf Common. Just £1000!

The highest attendance at any football match was 205,000, for the Brazil v Uruguay World Cup match in Rio de Janeiro on 16th July, 1950. A total of 136,505 fans watched Glasgow Celtic play Leeds United at Hampden Park, to establish the crowd-record for European Cup matches.

The record *paid* attendance for a British game – the Scotland v England International at Hampden Park in 1937 – is 149,547. But this total was probably exceeded on the occasion of the first F.A. Cup Final to be played at Wembley Stadium, between Bolton Wanderers and West Ham United. It is estimated that 160,000 fans swarmed into the stadium. The crush was so great that part of the crowd invaded the pitch, and delayed the start of the game by 40 minutes.

Those old rivals, Rangers and Celtic, inspired the highest attendance for a League match in Britain, when 118,567 watched them at Ibrox Park, Glasgow, on 2nd January, 1939.

In 1973, Goodison Park, Everton, was the scene of the lowest attendance for a British International, when only 4946 fans turned up to see Northern Ireland play Wales.

But the all-time 'low' for a Football League fixture is easily held by the 'crowd' that attended the Stockport County v Leicester City game at Old Trafford, Manchester, on 7th May, 1921. With Stockport's own ground under suspension, a grand total of 13 staunch enthusiasts watched the game!

## Longest and shortest . . .oldest and youngest

A match played between Santos (Brazil) and Penarol (Uruguay) is thought to be the longest recorded game of soccer. The marathon ended in a 3–3 draw, after the teams kicked off at 9.30 a.m. and played for $3\frac{1}{2}$ hours.

The longest F.A. Cup tie in the competition proper, between Stoke City and Bury, stretched over five games and 9 hours, 22 minutes of football. Stoke eventually won 3–2 in the final game.

Stoke also figured in one of the shortest games ever played, as far as individual players are concerned. Their striker, John Ritchie, was sent off during a 1972 U.E.F.A. Cup match against the West German club Kaiserslautern . . . 40 seconds after he had taken the field as substitute!

The longest continuous run in Division 1 of the Football League is claimed by Arsenal. They have not been relegated since they were elected in 1919.

Long, *unbeaten* runs are a feature of first-class football. Spurs won their first eleven games in 1960–61, which is the best start to a season by an English Football League First Division side.

In 1977–78, Nottingham Forest played 42 consecutive First Division games without defeat, easily beating the previous record by Leeds United (34).

The English League record for the longest run of consecutive *victories* (14), is shared by Bristol City (1905–06) and Preston North End (1950–51).

The Scottish League record belongs to Morton. They won 23 games in a row in Division 2, in 1963–64. Also in the Scottish League, Celtic played 63 games *without defeat* between November 1915 and April 1917 – another record for the 'Bhoys'.

Real Madrid can claim a really awesome 'longest'. Out of 122 *home* League games played between February 1957 and March 1965, they won 114 of them and drew 8. As if to underline their incredible soccer supremacy during this period, Real also won the European Cup four times!

The record for the 'longest' player to appear in a Football League match is held by Albert Iremonger, the Notts County and Leicester City goalkeeper. He was 6ft, 5ins tall. The shortest, at 5ft, was Fred Le May, who played for Watford and Clapton Orient from 1931 to 1933.

The *youngest* player to appear in the F.A. Cup competition was Scott Endersby. He was only fifteen years old when he played in goal for Kettering against Tilbury, in November 1977.

Manchester United's Duncan Edwards holds the record at International level, for an England player.

He was only eighteen years old when he played against Scotland in April 1955.

The *oldest* player to appear in an English Football League match was Neil McBain. He played in goal for New Brighton against Hartlepool in March 1947, at the age of 52.

But even International players live to a ripe old age, it seems. Billy Meredith was nearly 46 years of age when he played for Wales against England, on 15th March, 1920.

## Fastest

Bradford's Jim Fryatt claims the record for scoring the fastest goal in a Football League game. It's reported that he found the net against Tranmere Rovers only 4 seconds after the kick-off, on 25th August, 1964.

Other sources quote Albert Mundy of Aldershot as scoring the fastest goal on record, in 6 seconds, against Hartlepool United, in October 1958.

But an even more outrageous claim comes from Brazil. Whilst playing for Fluminense, Roberto Rivelino noticed that the opposing goalkeeper was still saying his pre-match prayers. Rather irreverently, you might think, Rivelino let fly, and gave his side a one-nil lead ... just 3½ seconds after the kickoff!

# 12 THE GREATEST GAME IN THE WORLD

You must have gathered by now that football is a very popular sport. Modern systems of communication, such as television, have helped to spread its influence to almost every corner of the earth.

Slowly, but surely, the soccer supremacy enjoyed for so long by Europe and South America is being challenged by the 'underdogs' of world football. In Africa and Asia, organised competitions are thriving at club and national level. And few visitors to the 1966 World Cup Finals will ever forget the sensational performances of little North Korea. Playing fast, exhilarating football, the Koreans disposed of mighty Italy 1–0, and romped to an astonishing 3–0 lead over Portugal in the quarter-finals. The relieved Portuguese eventually won 5–3, thanks mainly to the brilliance of their great striker, Eusebio.

In 1970, El Salvador and Morocco brought an exotic flavour to the Mexico finals, and four year later, in West Germany, Australia qualified for the first time, earning a creditable 0–0 draw with Chile. Australia failed to reach the Argentine finals, despite topping the Oceania qualifying group and adding Hong Kong and the Korean Republic to their list of victims. In Australia, soccer has to contend with fierce competition from Australian Rules Football, but the game is making steady progress. Perhaps the next World Cup tournament will see a stronger, more confident Australian team making another bid for the trophy. And perhaps, once again, they will be joined by Upper Volta, Senegal, Togo and Cameroon – just a few of the 96 countries which took part in the qualifying games, that culminated in 'Mundial 78', as the Argentinians called their World Cup finals.

But perhaps the most spectacular and intriguing

'boom' in the popularity of soccer is taking place in a country which failed to qualify for 'Mundial 78'.

## Soccer . . . American style

The American 'romance' with association football has come a long way since 1967, when leading clubs from Europe and South America were 'imported' and formed into leagues under completely different names. Hibernian became 'Toronto City', and Wolves (Los Angeles Wolves) beat Aberdeen (alias Washington Whips) 6–5 in one of the league finals.

Nowadays, with the help of high-powered salesmanship, top foreign players and a seemingly endless supply of dollars, soccer American-style is beginning to command the respect of the outside observers and officials who once dismissed it as a 'craze' that wouldn't last.

The North American Soccer League is organised into six divisions, stretching from the Canadian border in the north to Florida in the south-east. The individual clubs are owned and promoted by huge business concerns, and backed by rock stars such as Mick Jagger. So it's little wonder that they can afford the lucrative contracts which have attracted some of the best players in Europe and South America. Pele was the first of the soccer superstars to capture the imagination of the American public, when he signed for New York Cosmos. Other stars soon followed – Beckenbauer, George Best, Gordon Banks, Carlos Alberto of Brazil and Chinaglia from Italy. Trevor Francis of Birmingham City and England was reputedly paid £50,000 for little more than three months' football. In many cases, the clubs are managed and trained by former British professionals: men who are expected to build teams such as Tampa Bay Rowdies into respected clubs that will rank with the likes of

Arsenal and Real Madrid. And as you can see from the diagrams, the emblems of the American clubs are as spectacular and colourful as their names!

In fact, 'spectacle' and entertainment are the current keys to success in American soccer. To demonstrate this, let's pay an imaginary visit to a National Conference Eastern Division match between, say, New York Cosmos and Washington Diplomats.

One of the most pleasing features of American soccer is that an almost total absence of crowd trouble allows the whole family to go along to the game. And because the American sports promoter believes that the spectator is just as important as the player, you will probably be treated to a huge, mouth-watering barbecue in the stadium car park the moment you arrive!

Gorged to satisfaction, we move on into the stadium, which is furnished with comfortable seats. Not a concrete terrace in sight. The trim green pitch is surfaced with artificial 'astro' turf, and the mini-skirted girl cheer-leaders are already in action, whipping up support for their respective teams. Can you imagine such a thing happening at, say, Scunthorpe, on a chilly match-day in January? You wouldn't be able to see the girls for goose pimples!

But here in New Jersey the sun is shining, the bands are playing, and the huge, electronic score-boards are churning out 'commercials' on behalf of the firms that own or sponsor the clubs. Anything, in fact, to keep you amused until the players make their appearance, marching out on to the pitch like rows of modern gladiators.

After each player has been introduced individually, and praised to the skies, the match at last gets under way. And the accent is *still* on showmanship. Players are encouraged to show off their particular skills. Prolonged, defensive play is greeted with hoots and whistles of derision. You have come to see goals scored, which is why the off-side rule has been altered, to ensure that the ball hits the back of the net as many times as possible and to encourage attacking play.

At half-time there is no let-up in the entertainment. Amidst the snap and crackle of popcorn, clowns parade around the ground, trick motor-cyclists leap through blazing hoops, and stunt-men wrestle with alligators.

As the game continues, every exciting incident is

greeted at once with slogans such as 'Charge!' or 'Did See You That?', flashed on to the giant scoreboards. If this is a match which must produce a positive result – as is required in many American competitions – extra time will be played if the teams are level after 90 minutes – 7½ minutes each way. If the teams are still level at the end of extra time, keep your seats! Now comes the 'sudden death' finish ... a penalty 'shoot-out' between the rival players, to decide the overall winners. If your team has won, you'll roar with delight as the cheer-leaders go potty. And if you've supported the losers, at least you and your family will go home with the feeling that you have been thoroughly entertained.

'It's not the kind of 'entertainment' that meets with the entire approval of F.I.F.A. and other ruling bodies. But there is no doubt that the Americans are doing their best to make soccer take root in the U.S.A. The players are contractually bound to work on and off the field to promote the game and their club. They are expected to attend local community functions, open the odd restaurant or two, appear on 'chat' shows, and hold regular training sessions at schools and colleges. Rodney Marsh, the idol of Tampa Bay, has his own radio show.

But all this effort may be wasted if the American soccer scene continues to be dominated by foreign, 'imported' stars. Americans want success for *Americans*. If, within the next few years, the intensive training and coaching schemes fail to produce a powerful, all-American squad, strong enough to challenge for the world's major football honours, the average American sports fan will become more and more frustrated. His present passion for soccer may wither and die.

For the time being, however, soccer in America adds up to a colourful success story for all concerned. In August 1978, over 74,000 fans saw New York Cosmos retain their N.A.S.L. title by beating Tampa Bay Rowdies 3–1, with goals scored by Dennis Tueart (2) and Giorgio Chinaglia. Throughout the six American divisions, players who had been languishing in the reserves with British and European clubs have found undreamed-of success and stardom. And now it looks as if this same exciting process of soccer 'rags to riches' may be taking shape in the Middle East.

In the 1979 Arab Games in Baghdad, when the United Arab Emirates met Saudi Arabia in one of the first round matches, both of the opposing teams had been coached by British managers! An indication, perhaps, that the special 'charisma' of soccer can overcome the most difficult language barriers.

Like the Americans, the emerging Arab nations are prepared to pay – and pay handsomely – for the skill and experience that they need to mount a serious challenge in the arenas of world football. Foreign players, as well as managers, could well discover a new lease of life in the deserts of Arabia. With a little luck, a soccer-mad Sheik might even send for Pushy Pete.

So if you have a grain of soccer talent, for goodness' sake cherish it! For those who dedicate themselves to the game, the opportunities in soccer – on a world scale – are almost boundless. You will, of course, need the skill – earned through long hours of hard practice – to take advantage of these opportunities. Football is by no means an assured path to fame and riches. Apart from talent, you will also need humility – the ability to realise that success in any sport cannot be taken for granted.

Phil Parkes, who has written the foreword to this book, is a prime example of a successful player who learned from his own mistakes. Phil freely admits that his first taste of professional football, with Walsall, was a disaster. After missing training sessions because he couldn't be bothered to attend them, and revealing a general lack of dedication, he found himself pitched back into parks football at the age of fifteen. But from then on he got his head down, working hard at his game and his job as an apprentice carpenter. A year later, having realised that success in football does not come easily, Phil could have signed for Wolves, Birmingham City, West Bromwich Albion or Aston Villa ... but he chose to go back to Walsall. As a kind of personal challenge to himself, Phil wanted to make a fresh start with the club which had rejected him. This time, he did all the right things. At the age of eighteen he was transferred to Queens Park Rangers, where he became a permanent fixture 'between the sticks' until his transfer to West Ham United in February, 1979, for £565,000 – a world record for a goalkeeper.

Phil's personal experience is a story of success through dedication – a success that many of you might envy. No one can deny that it's nice to be famous, to be worshipped like players of the calibre of Pele and Cruyff. But if you are not good enough to become a professional footballer, there's nothing you can do about it, and there are millions like you.

All that matters, in the end, is that you do your best. Whether you play football or just watch it, keep your sense of humour. Keep cool, like Kevin, and honour soccer's codes of conduct.

Although soccer tends to take itself a little too seriously at times, it's still one of the greatest games in the world.

Enjoy it ... and be a credit to it.